Melissa Norton

JUST THE TWO OF US

Chandler House Press, Inc.
Worcester, Massachusetts

JUST THE TWO OF US

Copyright 2001 by Melissa Norton

Just the Two of Us

ISBN 1-886284-67-9
Library of Congress Card Number: 2001097341
First Edition
ABCDEFGHIJK

Published by
Chandler House Press, Inc.
A division of Tatnuck Bookseller & Sons, Inc.
335 Chandler Street
Worcester, MA 01602
USA

President
Lawrence J. Abramoff

Director of Publishing
Claire Cousineau

Cover & Interior Design
Patrick Mavros
Shoreline Graphics

Cover Photo
Patrick Mavros
Shoreline Graphics

Chandler House Press specializes in custom publishing for businesses,
organizations and individuals. For more information on how to publish
through our corporation, please contact Chandler House Press,
335 Chandler Street, Worcester, MA 01602. Call (800) 642-6657, fax (508) 756-9425,
or find us on the World Wide Web at www.chandlerhousepress.com.

JUST THE TWO OF US

For David

Introduction

David and I can't remember what made us first decide to try a three-day bike trip. Long-distance cycling was not a popular activity in the early 1970s. What we do remember is the first day of our maiden bike trip. We were excited as we pedaled away from David's parents' home in Fitchburg, Massachusetts. Our three young daughters, left in the care of their grandparents, waved us out of sight. It would be just the two of us for the next three days. We had a wonderful start. The weather was perfect—bright sunshine, warm temperature, low humidity. The rolling terrain was challenging, but doable. We both agreed that cycling was a wonderful way to spend time together. After lunch in Keene, New Hampshire, we turned north and our enthusiasm for the trip came to an abrupt halt. Tears ran down my face as I dismounted my bicycle to push it up Surrey Mountain. Rides around home had not included mountains. I was getting a taste of what long-distance cycling entailed and was rapidly coming to the conclusion that it was not for me. I loathed cycling as I continued pushing my bike up the steep grade. I wanted to go back home, but we were more than halfway to our destination. I vented my anger and frustration. "David, why are we doing this? You call this fun?" He, too, succumbed to the steep grade and got off his bike, but he walked ahead of me, not wanting to hear my complaints. Finally we reached the summit. I dried my tears and listened to David's encouraging words.

"I know you can make it, Melissa. We have a long downhill run ahead of us. Then it is just twenty miles." David was tired, but his confidence that we would achieve our goal never wavered.

Slowly we started our descent. We built up speed. The wind raced through my hair (this was in pre-helmet days). I loved the curves, leaning into them and then straightening up for a faster descent. As long as I didn't have to do the uphill part of a mountain, I thought long-distance cycling could be a fun activity. I loved going fast. I didn't want the downhill to end. As soon as we stopped at the base of Surrey Mountain, a police cruiser pulled up beside us. I was startled. What had we done? A smile came across the police officer's face as he asked, "Do you know you broke the speed limit?" We gave him a look of disbelief.

"I caught you on radar going thirty-seven miles an hour, and the posted speed limit is thirty-five," the officer told us, grinning. "I'll let you off this time, but please stay within the speed limit next time."

I wasn't sure there was going to be a next time. The downhill was fun, but I was tired, thirsty, hot, and not in the mood for more cycling. It's strange how your mind and body react when they have no other options. I wanted to quit, but I couldn't. There was no way for me to return home, except on a bicycle. Reaching our destination was the only option. When the clerk at a country store informed us the remainder of our route was flat, I forgot about our climb up Surrey Mountain. I forgot about how tired I was. I forgot about the heat. I focused on cycling.

The guests sitting on the porch of the inn in Springfield, Vermont stared at us as we biked in. I didn't care. I smiled, reveling in the knowledge I had just biked eighty-six miles. And they weren't easy miles.

Back in the early 1970s, arriving at a country inn on a bicycle was unusual. Perhaps that was the cause of the stares we received from the guests. Or maybe it was our unique luggage that caught their attention: brown paper grocery bags. We secured them with rope in our rear-mounted child seats. The stares stopped when the guests learned of our long ride. They treated us like heroes. We didn't have to buy a single beer!

When we got to our room I rushed to the phone. I needed to call my parents and friends to tell them we completed the first day of our three-day trip. My adrenaline was on overdrive.

David was also thrilled with our accomplishment but was too occupied to call anyone. As I spoke with his mother, David shouted from the bathroom, "Tell her we made it and I'll call her later." He was seeking relief in a tub of hot water. His butt was too sore to put back on a bicycle seat. The firm leather saddle had caused blisters to form on his tender backside. (I carry extra natural padding in that area, so I didn't suffer to the extent David did.) The next day, David draped several washcloths over his bicycle seat and held them secure with masking tape. By the time he finished wrapping the seat, it looked like a fully stuffed cushion. The doctored saddle allowed David to finish the trip. We rode 256 miles on that first outing.

David is a practicing management consultant and the co-author of the books *The Balanced Scorecard* and *The Strategy-Focused Organization,* and I am a retired teacher of mathematics and computer science. Our cycling careers began on Christmas Day, 1970, when we were twenty-nine years old. That holiday, we presented each other with Schwinn bicycles, British racing green in color. The technology of cycling was advancing. Our new bikes had three speeds, and the tires were thin, compared to the balloon tires of the one-speeds we rode as youngsters. The brake levers on the Schwinns were on the handlebars, allowing for both rear and front braking, adding convenience and a greater level of safety. Gone were the foot brakes a cyclist once relied on, engaging them by reversing direction on the pedals.

Installed on David's bike were an infant seat on the crossbar and a child seat over the rear wheel. My bike had only a rear child seat. Each evening during the following summer, we would ride to an ice cream shop in the next town, a round trip of ten miles. Our daughters, looking forward to a nightly ice cream, encouraged our cycling.

It was Memorial Day weekend, 1972, when David and I took the first of what became many three-day bike trips. When he planned the trip, David reasoned that if on our nightly ice cream runs we covered ten miles in one hour, we could cover eighty miles in eight hours. With those numbers in mind he pulled out maps and selected a route that covered approximately eighty miles per day. On the map the trip looked feasible. That is why I consented to accompany him.

On that first trip we learned many things. Seeing the countryside at ten miles an hour was a new and wonderful experience. As we slowly rolled through a landscape of red barns, bright green fields, and distant mountains, we felt we were a part of it—much more so than we ever had. We learned to recognize the smell of newly turned soil, of dairy cattle grazing on hillsides, and of rushing water in roadside streams. Feeling the fresh air engulf us as we pedaled along was a joy. Our exercise-induced appetite gave food new meaning—everything tasted superb! We also liked our feeling of accomplishment. We were proud of those 256 miles. We arrived home with sore butts and tired legs, but had nothing but praise for our first cycling adventure.

After that first trip, a tradition was born. Each Memorial Day weekend we took a three-day cycling trip. Laying out the trips was David's task. First he would find places to stay. (Country inns with their own dining facilities were our favorite.) Then he would map out a route between accommodations, trying to get in eighty-plus miles per day. On those weekend trips we traveled through the Berkshires of Massachusetts. We cycled long valleys and climbed steep gaps in Vermont. We explored coastal roads in Maine. We cycled past ski areas in New Hampshire. And we learned about being long-distance cyclists.

Each spring, prior to our annual trip, we got ourselves into cycling shape. As soon as the winter snows receded, we were out cycling. We bought multi-geared bikes to give us the low range of gears necessary for hill climbing. We stopped using shopping bags for luggage, replacing them with rear racks and panniers. We stopped using candy and soda for sustenance, learning about high-energy drinks and healthy food. Our biking attire evolved to include padded shorts. We added cold weather clothing and rain apparel to our gear. We were becoming serious cyclists!

Each year we looked forward to our 3-day bike trip. As we approached our fiftieth birthdays in 1991, we thought, "Why not celebrate our half-century of life with a longer trip?" David got out his guidebooks and maps and planned a two-week trip covering one thousand miles. The plan was to cycle across Massachusetts, to the rolling hills of New York State. At Rochester, New York, we would reverse course, cycle past Lake Ontario, cross the northern tip of Lake Champlain, and travel south through Vermont back to our home in Massachusetts. We were apprehensive about covering that distance. Could we grind out long cycling days for two weeks? On that trip we braved stiflingly hot weather. We rode through torrential downpours. From a cyclist at one of our stops, we learned that some of the steep, rolling terrain we cycled was part of a training ride for Olympic cyclists. Most importantly, we discovered we loved being on the road. We came home from our first two-week trip ready to plan the next one. A seed had been planted. We knew that, given the time, we could accomplish a cross-country ride. What we needed was time!

But with our busy schedules, time was not easy to come by. In each subsequent year we took another two-week trip. Our second was from Jackson Hole, Wyoming to Seattle, Washington. The third trip began in Jackson Hole, Wyoming, traveled through the Rocky Mountains, and terminated in Durango, Colorado. Our fourth trip took us from Vancouver, British Columbia to Banff, Alberta, continuing through Glacier National Park in Montana. In June of 1995, as we trained for our fifth trip, cycling around the island of Nova Scotia, our biking came to a sudden halt.

On a twenty-mile training run I hit a sizable rock. The bike and I landed in the center of the road. My first recollection was looking up in the ambulance and seeing a former student of mine. "Rick! What are you doing here?" I asked. Smiles circulated around the emergency crew. If I recognized Rick, I probably didn't have a concussion, although the shell of my helmet was cracked. After numerous tests at the hospital, it was determined that none of my bones was broken, although my body had many abrasions. The major injury was a large hematoma on my right hip, which caused a deep bruise the length of my right leg. A daily regimen of aquatic physical therapy replaced summer cycling. Our active lifestyle came to an end. David took up golf.

During the following winter, disaster hit again. In the space of one month, I was involved in two ski accidents, one causing injury to my right shoulder, the other to my right knee. In short order, I was becoming an orthopedic surgeon's ideal patient. In March I awoke from surgery on my shoulder to hear the doctor say, "It was a bit worse than I expected." Instead of returning home with a sling, I carried my right arm at a forty-five-degree angle, supported by a foam wedge lodged in my armpit. I could do nothing with my arm in that position; I couldn't bathe, I couldn't sleep. It was easy to feel depressed. I tried to keep my spirits up, but gnawing at me was the knowledge I had another operation to undergo. I had completed only the first act of a two-act play. I faithfully did physical therapy, and by August my shoulder was strong enough to support crutches, so I could get on with act two, having the anterior cruciate ligament in my right knee reconstructed. As I lay in the pre-op room with a sedative dripping into my veins, I whispered, "Here I go again!" and tears flowed freely.

My accidents affected David, too. He missed having me as a companion in his various activities. He gave up his ski season as soon as I was injured. Bike rides alone were not as much fun, and he took fewer of them. Life was slowing down for both of us.

As I recovered from the second surgery, I kept reminding myself that with time we could regain the active lifestyle we once enjoyed. I needed to focus on that because recovery from major knee surgery takes time and work. Meanwhile, I fought with my body and my mind. I didn't want my body wearing out, and I didn't want my mind dwelling on self-pity. For my body I did physical therapy. For my mind David offered me a challenge.

Soon after I returned home from the second surgery, David sat next to me on the bed and said, "Next summer, let's do it. Let's cycle across the United States!"

"Yeah, right!" I answered. "I've heard that before. Remember two years ago when we started to plan and how quickly the plans fell through?"

"Seriously, Melissa, there is no better time for us to do this. It's time to make this a reality. No more dreaming. I'm informing my colleagues at work I am taking nine weeks off next summer."

David knew what he was doing. He was getting my mind into the recovery process. He gave me a goal. He gave me something to dream about, to anticipate, to plan for. The carrot was dangling in front of me: get yourself ready to cycle across the United States!

Soon both of us were discussing the route we would follow for our trip. David purchased guidebooks and road maps and had me search the Internet. We discussed places we wanted to see. South Dakota was a state we wanted on our itinerary; we also wanted to do some cycling along the Mississippi River. Each day we got more into the planning process. We spread a large United States map on a table in our den, and David started penciling in our route.

We approached the cross-country trip from different perspectives. David insisted the trip be an athletic challenge, with 100-mile-plus days included. I wanted days off so we could rent a car and see sights beyond our planned itinerary. But we did agree on one thing: we would do no camping out. After a long day on a bicycle, we both wanted a hot shower and a good meal. Finding good accommodations and the best restaurant in town became two of our requisites. With these parameters in place, the real planning process began.

The prevailing winds across the United States come from the west, and we took advantage of this, planning the trip from the West

Coast to the East. Adventure Cycling, a national bicycling organization in Missoula, Montana, provided most of the maps for the trip. The organization has three planned routes for cross-country bicycle travel: a northern route, a central route, and a southern route. The maps are geared toward the "camping" cyclist, avoiding large cities and main roads. We used their central tier maps to plan our trip from Oregon to Yellowstone National Park. From Wyoming to Indiana, we left Adventure Cycling's routes and created our own, using maps from travel bookstores and the U. S. Coast and Geodesic Service. For the route from central Indiana to Maine, we returned to Adventure Cycling's maps, using their northern tier route. The Internet also proved a good resource. We found a web page that had an itinerary we used for several weeks of our trip.

David spent many evenings with the maps, charting our trip. He tried to locate cities and towns large enough to have accommodations, and close enough to one another to cycle from one to the next. He used guidebooks, tourist information bureaus, and even phone calls to park rangers in remote locations of the West to find accommodations for nine weeks on the road. The completed itinerary, sixty-three days, would take us from Astoria, Oregon to Bar Harbor, Maine, an estimated distance of 4,500 miles. It included nine layover days in places we thought would be interesting. It was up to me to make reservations for those nine weeks on the road.

I spent much of January on the phone, calling inns, bed-and-breakfasts, motels and hotels. When I made a reservation I told the clerk to be sure to hold the room, because we would be on bicycles. The response I received ranged from delight to disbelief. Invariably the clerk asked from where we would be biking. If I received the response, "That is far away. You can't ride that in a day," I would run to David and complain about the itinerary.

"The reservationist says that is an impossible distance for a cyclist. Don't you think you should recheck the mileage?"

David was always reassuring. "Remember, Melissa, you are probably talking to people who don't bike. They don't know how much distance you can cover in a day."

Another response I received when I told them we would be on bikes was, "Oh, you are on motorcycles."

"No, *we* are providing the power."

When the clerk at a New York inn learned we were on bikes, she became very excited. "Oh, we love to have cyclists. I suppose you want to stay in our bunk room behind the back stairs, where there are beds for six, sharing a bath. I remember you cyclists love peanut butter. I'll have plenty on hand for you." When I told her we preferred a private room with a bath, she said we weren't like her other cycling guests. "However," I assured her, "we love peanut butter."

Another important part of the planning process was checking to see if dining was available at each overnight stop. Just as a car needs fuel, a touring cyclist needs food—lots of food.

By February, our planning process was complete. Our next goal was to get into strong cycling shape.

Being in shape is something David has worked at all his life. He was a runner long before it was fashionable. He remembers running in sneakers, before the advent of the "running shoe." He joined softball teams at work. On weekends he played handball and tennis. And he biked. Being physically fit is a natural state for David.

I, on the other hand, was late to join the fitness crowd. Each spring, I would bike to work, a round-trip of twelve miles, to prepare for our annual three-day ride. The rest of the year, I did nothing except walk the dogs and chase after our active daughters. When I turned 35, David presented me with a challenge. "I bet you can't run a mile."

"Of course I can run a mile," I replied.

He gave me a mile course, and I set out. Only my competitive nature got me to finish that first grueling mile. I ached for days, but after that I started to run on a daily basis. I enjoyed the increase in energy running gave me.

After turning 40, I added weight lifting to my fitness regimen. Our daughters, on the recommendation of their swim coach, had started doing Nautilus weight training. While the girls did their rotations on the weight machines, I sat and read a magazine. One day the manager of the Nautilus center asked me why I didn't join my daughters in a weight-lifting program. My excuse, "I'd be the only adult woman in here" was too shallow for him. He offered a free session to teach me how to use the various pieces of equipment. Once started, I was faithful to my weight-lifting schedule. What kept me lifting was the rapid, positive change in my appearance. My inherited pear shape was shrinking. People noticed my slimmer appearance, although I had put on several pounds of muscle. I had become as committed as David to keeping myself fit.

In selecting bikes for our trip, we chose Trek 520 touring models. David had the standard gearing replaced with one that had a higher top gear and a lower bottom gear, providing a broader range. We knew we would need the lower gear for sustained hill climbing but David also wanted the higher gear so we could pedal on the down-hills, getting maximum speed.

On previous bike trips we'd encountered roads that were under construction or were not paved at all. We would slow down to cycle on them, hoping we wouldn't get a flat tire from the rough surface. For this trip, to protect us on all types of road surfaces, we selected Continental cross-country tires. Their wider treads and thicker skins offered greater stability on all surfaces—loose gravel, soft sand, newly paved macadam.

For years, we've used panniers for carrying our gear—each of us using two rear-mounted packs and one handlebar bag. On this trip I opted for a different method to carry my belongings.

While walking my daughter's dog in California, I noticed a lanky cyclist pedaling by, his bright yellow shirt visible for blocks. He was pulling a carrier that was attached to the rear hub of his bike. It was made of meshed metal, and was approximately three feet long, a foot and a half wide and a foot deep with a small, centered wheel attached to the rear. Inserted in the carrier was a duffel bag. I called out, "Hey, can you stop for a minute?"

Hearing me, he looked up from his bent over position. He made a wide turn in the road and pulled up beside me.

"Hi, I'm Jim. What can I do for you?"

"I've seen those carriers advertised in biking magazines. Are they really good for hauling gear?" I inquired.

"It's a B.O.B. carrier and they're great for carrying stuff. Want to try it? Why don't you take a spin around the neighborhood?"

"OK," I replied, as I handed him the dog's leash.

Jim's bike was too big for me. I had to stretch to reach the pedals. Cautiously, I pulled into the road, loaded B.O.B. carrier in tow. I wasn't comfortable on the large bike, but as soon as I maneuvered around the first corner, I knew I would give up panniers. I never felt out of balance as I leaned into the curve the way I would have if I had been carrying heavy panniers.

When I returned from my test ride, I was smiling.

"What do you think?" asked Jim. I dismounted and gave him two thumbs up.

"It's great!"

"I should work for B.O.B. carrier. My cycling partner has ordered one, and now you've been sold."

We lingered awhile, talking about the B.O.B. and our upcoming bike trips—his along the coast of Oregon and mine, the trans-America.

David meticulously planned our cross-country itinerary, and he applied the same attention to detail to decide what gear he would take.

Upon returning home from other bike trips, he would eliminate items he had brought along that he decided were not necessary. Throughout the years, he has created a detailed list of what to take on cycling trips—from tools to biking attire to off-the-bike clothes. All his planning was done to minimize the weight he carried. David referred to this list as he compiled his gear for our cross-country trip.

I never made such a list.

Perhaps it is my feminine side that won't let me wear the same biking clothes two days in a row. We planned to do laundry at least every fourth day so I carried four sets of biking shorts and shirts. I also carried two "nice" outfits, three sets of casual shorts and tops, a bathing suit, several T-shirts, jeans, sneakers, dress shoes, casual shoes and a full complement of cold weather biking gear and rainwear. I had clothes to cover any situation. This was not going to be like our other bike trips. We were going to be on the road for nine weeks. I knew I had more gear than on previous trips, but I thought carrying the extra weight would be easier with the B.O.B. carrier. David kept telling me, "Weight is weight. Your legs still have to get it over the hills." He didn't convince me to lighten my load.

Spring found us cycling whenever possible. The weather was cold and rainy. We cycled anyway. On a planned coast-to-coast itinerary such as ours, we had to cycle no matter what the weather. We tested our rain gear. We tested our cold-weather gear. We tested our lights for night cycling. We tested ourselves. We felt we were ready for our coast-to-coast trip.

When we told friends and family about our planned cross-country bike trip, we were greeted with skepticism. One of our sons-in-law boldly inquired, "Isn't that a bit much? I know you like to cycle, but at your age do you think you can do it?" Age hadn't entered our thinking. We are not baby boomers, although David likes to think we are. He likes to say "we are on the leading edge of that large post-World War II generation," referring to the members of the population bubble who continue to push back the onset of middle-age, attempting to maintain the active lifestyles of their youth. Truthfully, we were born in 1941, before the start of the baby boom. As we contemplated our trip, we were determined to prove our son-in-law and all other skeptics wrong. The two of us, well into middle age but fit, would cycle across America.

The following pages reveal my journal notes and observations as we pedaled along the byways of America. I have included maps and our daily itinerary. David had an odometer that recorded how much elevation gain (hill climbing) we achieved each day, along with our mileage. For fellow cyclists I've noted these numbers, so the ease or difficulty of a day will be more apparent.

Chapter 1

Coast Ranges of Oregon

		Miles	Elevation Gain (ft.)
June 13	Fly to Portland, Oregon	-	-
June 14	Travel to Astoria, Oregon	-	-
June 15	Tillamook, Oregon	71	3,100
June 16	Salem, Oregon	112	4,900
June 17	Eugene, Oregon	85	1,100
June 18	Redmond, Oregon	113	5,600
June 19	Prineville, Oregon	43	810
June 20	John Day, Oregon	117	5,070
June 21	Baker City, Oregon	82	4,780
June 22	Baker City	Layover Day	

MILEAGE: 623 / ELEVATION GAIN: 25,360 FEET

June 13

Tomorrow is the day we start our cross-country journey. After spending hours examining maps, David has our route. We have read books by other cyclists who have done the cross-country ride. We have room reservations for nine weeks on the road. Bills have been prepaid. House, garden and pet care is scheduled. All items on the pre-trip list are checked off. We just need to get to Astoria, Oregon, where we will claim our bikes, sent by airfreight ten days ago. After a year of planning, we are ready to start our trip cycling across the United States.

Our first stop will be the Pacific Ocean. Cyclists making a coast-to-coast trip share a tradition. Before starting, they dip their rear bike wheels into the Pacific Ocean and upon reaching the Atlantic Ocean, they roll their front wheels into the sea. As soon as we dip our wheels, we'll put the Pacific Ocean to our backs and start our journey.

Our minds are filled with questions. Can we do this trip? Can we cope with mishaps? Can we tolerate each other's company for such a long time? As we embark on this journey, we hope to have good weather, smooth roads, and strong tailwinds.

June 14

Last evening, we arrived in Portland, Oregon. As I stepped from the cab and saw the elegant Benson Hotel, I almost forgot why we were here. The four-star hotel, with many amenities, is designed for relaxation. The young porter who removed our panniers and duffel from the cab quickly reminded us of our upcoming journey.

"Where are you cycling? How long will you be on the road?" His interest in our trip continued as we moved into the lobby. As a fellow cyclist he wanted to get as many details as possible in the short time it took us to check in.

As we unpacked we kept telling ourselves we were about to start the trip we had been planning and anticipating for close to a year. Tomorrow we would be in Astoria, the city with the first red dot on our large United States map. Green dots on the map indicated our daily stops. Not another red dot appeared until the finish in Bar Harbor. Red dot to red dot. Could we—two middle-age cyclists—do it? Would my knee hold up under the strain of daily cycling? The next few weeks would give us the answer.

At breakfast we didn't linger over coffee. We were anxious to get started. Using a one-way rental car, we proceeded to Astoria.

For months David had searched guidebooks looking for interesting places to stay for our nine weeks on the road. As we reached the top of a hill in Astoria and saw the Rosebriar Inn, we knew his research for Astoria was successful. The Inn was a large Victorian house with a front porch overlooking the town and the mouth of the Columbia River. There were flower gardens rimming the house and the porch had several wooden chairs inviting us to sit and enjoy the view. As we stepped into the front parlor, we saw vases filled with fresh flowers, wooden floors and stairs polished to a high gloss, and a reception parlor decorated in a simple, tasteful manner. As soon as we were shown to our room, we changed into biking attire to spend the afternoon on our bikes exploring Astoria.

Our first stop was the edge of the Columbia River, where we watched as fishermen reeled in three- to four-foot-long sturgeon. The camaraderie of the anglers as they shouted to one another, "Nice catch!" or "That one must have been difficult to land!" led me to believe this was a daily regimen. The dockside group shared beers, conversation, and the mutual happiness generated by a good catch.

At the Astoria tourist center, we met several touring cyclists. A natural bond exists among cyclists. David and I think it comes from "knowing your pain"—we all have stories to tell about tough hills, bad weather, and irate drivers. We discovered most of the cyclists at the tourist center were European, and none was embarking on a trip across the United States. All the cyclists we spoke with were heading down the coast to Argentina. Most were cycling in groups, but we spoke to a young German woman who was cycling the Pacific coast, from Alaska to Argentina, alone. She was happy to engage us in conversation. We discussed her solitary cycling adventure and our upcoming travels. We learned she had been on the road for several weeks, and her enthusiasm for her lengthy trip had not waned. It gave us hope as we started our journey.

We waited our turn to ask the gracious, elderly woman on duty at the information desk where we could get the best view of the Columbia River as it empties into the Pacific Ocean. "That's easy," replied the woman. "You're on bikes, right? I hope you like to climb hills because the best view is from Astoria Tower. You'll have to climb Coxcomb

Hill to get there." As soon as we stepped onto the tower's observation deck and saw the 360-degree view, we agreed the climb was worth it. We saw snaking rivers, angular hills and deeply cut valleys, all linked to the Columbia River that has been eroding the land for millennia. A plaque on the tower's observation deck informed us we were overlooking Fort Clapsop, the wintering quarters of Lewis and Clark in 1805–6. It was the first of many encounters we would have with the explorers.

Whenever David and I travel, we try to find restaurants that offer local cuisine, rather than eating in national chains. As we cycled along Astoria's main street I noticed a storefront bistro called Ira's. With time on our hands, we stopped. The glowing restaurant review posted in the window convinced us this might be a restaurant to try, so we stepped inside. A large deli-style cooler of cold cuts and salads confronted us. "Is this the place described in the review posted on the window?" I asked in surprise. Ira's mother, sitting in a chair next to the cooler, quickly responded, "You walked into the deli part of the business. Next-door is our restaurant. We serve the best food in Astoria…I promise you! You eat here, you go home happy!" She directed my attention to a cozy room on her left where red chairs were set around white-clothed tables. Ira, the chef, the owner, and the waiter, joined the marketing ploy and said he personally guaranteed we would enjoy our dinners. How could we refuse? We booked dinner at Ira's.

For starters we had freshly shucked oysters from the Pacific Ocean. To prove the freshness of the mollusks, Ira pointed out the window to a promontory. "That's where your oysters were harvested," he said. With little need of convincing from Ira, we ordered Northwestern salmon for an entrée, a special treat for us Easterners. Ira took his job seriously. He helped deliver each course, and he hovered nearby, waiting to get our review of the food. Ira wanted us to be satisfied. "Was the salmon cooked to your taste?" "Save room for dessert, my specialty." We were not disappointed. As we lingered over berry-filled pastries, we made plans for our early morning start and the beginning of our adventure.

June 15

Sunrise—it was time to go. We were barely into our morning ride when we realized that the Oregon coast is steep, rolling terrain. David, who has complete confidence in his cycling ability, never doubted we would make our destination for the day. I did not share in his faith. Was the tough terrain going to beat me? Would I have to walk hills on the first day? As I struggled up the hills, I questioned if I had trained enough. We had done most of our training without baggage, and now we carried gear. Our legs were not used to the extra weight. As we pushed up the hills, I questioned David. "Are these hills really steep or am I just not in good shape?"

"They're steep, but you can do it." I noticed David was also having trouble with the hills. Both of us continued to turn our cranks, bearing down hard on the pedals, and made the hills.

On previous bike trips, whenever we'd chatted with other touring cyclists, they'd often bragged they had done the Oregon coast. And now we know why. Those cyclists deserve their badges of courage! Uphill, downhill, no flat stretches. Fortunately, the views over the Pacific Ocean made the climbs rewarding. Sheer cliffs rise from the water and large, rugged rock formations jut through the surf. The moist, sweet ocean air and the pink and purple sweet pea cascading over roadside shrubs kept my senses busy. Even though the terrain was difficult, I cycled in a state of euphoria, excited to be on our way.

Our first night on the road we spent in Tillamook, a coastal town known for its cheese. As we were pedaling the last few miles into town, a car towing a fishing boat tooted at us. We cheerily waved to the driver and gave it no further thought. As we continued down the road, we noticed the car towing the boat was parked on the side of the road, and the driver was flagging us down. As we got closer, we realized it was Riley, a friend who moved to the Portland area years ago. He and his wife were spending time at their summer cottage on the coast. They knew our itinerary and had hoped they would find us along the road. Riley was excited his search had paid off. We chatted for a while and made plans to meet for dinner.

Meanwhile, our daughter Stephanie and her family were driving up from the San Francisco area to give us a send-off. Shortly after we'd checked into our room and showered, we heard the phone ring. "Gammy, Pops, it's me, Trés. Where are you?" We gave them the room number, and in moments we were swooping our two young grandchildren into our arms. Our exhaustion melted away as we listened to their happy babble.

It was a large, noisy group that dined at the Shilo Inn that evening. Everyone toasted us, giving us their best wishes for a successful trip. As I smiled and joked with the group, what went through my mind was, "One day down; sixty-two to go." And the first day had not been easy! If we were going to complete this trip, we would need everyone's best wishes along with luck, determination, and strength—both physical and emotional.

June 16

We awoke to a heavy fog and continued our travels along the coast, unable to see the ocean. Only our brightly colored rain jackets allowed us to see each other. Without the imposing ocean views to divert our attention, the rolling hills seemed longer and felt steeper. By mid-morning the fog had lifted, and we got our final look at the Pacific Ocean. The heavy, cloud-covered sky made the water look cold, dark and ominous. The air above the water's surface was still laden with moisture, and we could feel it engulf us as it moved onshore.

On the recommendation of our Portland friends, we stopped in the coastal town of Pacific City to have breakfast at a restaurant called the Grateful Bread. Patrons leaving the restaurant gave us a quick preview of the meal to come. They recommended we try the challah French toast, which came smothered in a fresh raspberry-apple compote. It was a great choice. My taste buds awoke as I took the first bite of the crusty, thick bread with the soft, moist, egg-filled center. Usually I eat rapidly, but for this taste sensation, I slowed down. I didn't want the experience to end. Finally, I swallowed the last bite, sat back, and sipped my coffee. My hunger satisfied, I had a chance to look around the Grateful Bread. It was more art gallery than restaurant, its walls lined with the work of local artists. Several pieces caught my eye, but we didn't have time to dally over paintings. I got one artist's business card, and we hit the road again.

After leaving Pacific City, we turned east, putting the coast forever behind us, and started our ascent of the coastal mountains. In Oregon the lower Coast Ranges are covered with "Doug fir" (the locals' description of the majestic Douglas fir tree). Our route passed through an old-growth forest where the trees were draped with dried hanging moss and the forest floor was carpeted with lush green ferns. The expansive canopy of the towering fir trees blocked out the sun; only an occasional ray of sunshine streamed through to illuminate the soft ferns. As we pedaled upward, we felt we were cycling through a moist, dark tunnel.

It was a long day. Our final odometer reading was 112 miles. We were exhausted as we rolled into Salem and started looking for our night's accommodations. As tired as we were, we had reason to be happy. We could feel ourselves getting into stronger cycling shape. The hills were getting easier to climb. The only problem we had was sore, tender butts. We were regularly applying K-Y lubricating jelly, as recommended by an experienced long-distance cyclist, but our backsides were still sensitive. It would take a few more days in the saddle to alleviate the pain.

We were pleasantly surprised as we rode up the driveway of the Marquee House, a stately inn tucked away on a quiet street one block from the main thoroughfare of Salem. The inn had a large verandah, surrounded by a perennial garden beautifully cared for by the innkeeper. An inviting lawn sloped off to a rushing brook. It was the perfect setting for two weary cyclists. We relaxed next to the stream, dangling our feet in the frigid water, consuming thirst-quenching beers and recounting the events of the day.

Biking, even with a companion, is solitary. It is comforting to look ahead and know you are sharing the experience, but unless you are taking a break, you don't talk with your partner. Sometimes I got frustrated enough to shout tidbits of conversation to David, but I knew most of it went unheard. (At least it was never acknowledged!) Upon completing a day we found it necessary to catch up. It became a daily ritual—reviewing the day over several beers.

Each of the guest rooms in the Marquee House is decorated around a movie theme. The innkeeper, a movie buff and avid collector of cinematic memorabilia, had trinkets and paraphernalia from scores of old movies lining the walls and bookcases. We were directed to the garden-side Auntie Mame room, where broad-brimmed, plumed hats decorated with silk flowers and shiny beads were ceremoniously placed on bureaus. Display cases of gaudy rhinestone necklaces and bracelets sat in every corner. The large walk-in closet was filled with elegant evening gowns and sophisticated daytime ensembles—all with coordinating shoes or boots. Stylishly draped over the arm of a chair were long white evening gloves—a pearl encrusted evening bag placed next to them. Partygoer Mame would have been delighted to stay here.

As we explored the inn, peeking into other guest rooms and guessing their movie themes, we discovered the innkeeper had placed us in the wrong room. With our tender backsides we should have been directed to the room based on the movie *Blazing Saddles.*

June 17

We crossed the Coast Ranges and entered Willamette Valley, the destination of the settlers who traveled the Oregon Trail. Large farms covered the valley: vineyards, bulb and flower nurseries, and cattle ranches. As we cycled the lengthy valley, we smelled a sweet, familiar fragrance. Field after field was planted with the aromatic crop. What was it? Finally, we found a farm whose fields were labeled, and our mystery was solved: peppermint.

The road was flat and we were making great time as we headed into Eugene, a college town in the valley. We looked forward to spending the afternoon exploring Eugene's downtown area. Then it happened. Bang! The sound of breaking glass and then that dreaded hiss. I hadn't seen the glass beer bottle in my path, and my rear wheel ran over it. As I pulled off to the side of the road, I saw my back tire was shredded. Our first blowout! David, meticulous about planning, had made sure each of us carried a spare tire—one that had thin treads and canvas-like sidewalls. The tire was designed to be used for emergency situations. When planning the trip, we chose to bring this type of tire because it folds for easy storage. A "real" tire is rigid and would have been difficult to carry. Our thinking was: How often do you ruin a tire? Inner tubes may need replacement. But tires? Not often. We felt an emergency tire would last us long enough to get to a bike store.

Because we were almost in Eugene, David decided to go to a bike shop to purchase a "real" tire, saving our fold-up tires for another emergency. Two young boys on bikes, who stopped to ask if we needed help, directed us to a bike shop several miles away. David rode ahead to buy a new tire. Meanwhile, I sat by the side of the road and typed information into the journal I was keeping on my palm-sized computer. Computers are everywhere, but using one while sitting on a curb beside a busy highway near Eugene, Oregon may be a first.

In selecting a computer for the trip, I had three requirements. First, it needed to have a keyboard for fast input of information. Second, it had to have the capability to access e-mail. And, third, it couldn't weigh more than a pound. Apple Computer's MessagePad met all my requirements and I purchased one. A padded, zippered pouch protected the small computer as it traveled in my B.O.B. carrier.

Dick Nolan, a business colleague of David's, upon hearing of our planned TransAmerica trip, insisted I let his son, Sean, host a Web page for us. At first I declined, stating I wasn't sure I wanted to share my thoughts over the Internet. Dick kept after me. "Melissa, what you and David are doing is special. A lot of us want to follow as you cycle across the country."

Finally, Dick persuaded me. I now had an Internet audience to address. The plan was to have me send Sean e-mail describing our journey. He would then post the information on our Web page. A simple plan, but it required me to keep up with my writing.

At dinner that evening, we discussed the next day's ride. We were going to climb McKenzie Pass through the Cascade Range. It was our longest and steepest climb in Oregon, 21 miles and reaching an elevation of 5,324 feet above sea level. David looked forward to the challenge. I was anxious about the long climb.

A decade ago I was diagnosed with exercise-induced asthma. Instead of expanding as I push myself physically, answering my body's need for more oxygen, the airways in my lungs constrict. An asthma attack is the result. When I told my doctor about our bike trip, he said I should be fine as long as I take my medications on a regular basis. I've learned over the years that the best approach to sustained climbing is to put my bike in its lowest gear before the grade gets too steep and then to concentrate on a slow, steady breathing pattern. I let my leg muscles do the work, not my lungs. On some hills, I've seen my odometer drop to three miles an hour as I concentrate on my breathing.

David understands why I get anxious before we attempt a long climb. As a young man he suffered from asthma, although he no longer does. He remembers what it's like to struggle for a breath of air. Putting a lighter side to the health issue, he sometimes joked, "At least we're keeping it in the family."

At stops David asked me, "Have you taken your asthma stuff?" As a cycling team, we both were concerned about asthma attacks.

So, while David quickly dropped into slumber, I tossed and turned, worried about the long climb ahead.

June 18

David and I packed up in the predawn light outside the River Valley Inn, in the company of airline crews having to make an early flight. All of us were getting our first dose of nutrition—coffee. Getting up in the dark was difficult and caffeine was mandatory to get the body moving. After downing a large cup of the strong brew, we left Eugene behind and commenced a slow climb along the McKenzie River.

It was a beautiful morning. Traffic was light. The river was flowing rapidly, filled with spring snowmelt. I was happy cycling along, watching the river flow by, losing myself in my thoughts. Most of them focused on how fortunate David and I were to both love long-distance cycling. We rolled along in unison. As I looked ahead, I saw that reassuring sight—David hunkered down over his bike, his legs pumping the pedals. Many married couples "awaken" from their child-rearing years to discover they no longer share interests. For years the main focus of the marriage has been child rearing; then suddenly, the children are gone. Now what? One partner likes the theater, the other sailing. One likes golf, the other reading. David and I think we avoided this "later life" dilemma because during our dating years, we discovered we both like the outdoors and that formed the foundation of a lifetime of shared interests. As teenagers, we took long walks. We picnicked by roadside streams. We went skiing. Later on, as I became more fit, cycling became a natural sport for us to enjoy together. As we sped along the McKenzie River, I was grateful I had a companion to share the experience with.

At noon we reached the base of McKenzie Pass. We stopped at a country store to add snacks and drinks to our packs, knowing services would be nonexistent until we descended the other side of the pass and rode into Sisters, Oregon. We questioned the clerk about the mountain pass.

"The pass is still closed," she informed us.

"Can we get through on bicycles?"

"I'm sure you can," she replied. "The road was plowed last week. But you'll probably find windblown snow on the road near the summit."

"When does the road open?" I inquired.

"Not until July 4th for cars. Right now, only walkers and cyclists are allowed. Partway up you'll notice a large gate that stops cars from going up the road."

What great news! No automobiles, no motorcycles and best of all, no wide, lengthy RVs to compete with as we climbed the pass.

We have climbed many hills in our cycling careers, some short and steep, others long and gradual. To break the monotony of hill climbing, David and I have each created little games. Doing quick mathematical calculations is one of David's innate skills. The accounting people at his office marvel at how quickly he can estimate percentages of growth or decline as he scans a set of numbers. David applies this skill to our hill climbing. For the trip David purchased a new odometer equipped with an altimeter. As we started a climb, he would note our altitude in feet. For example, we would begin at 1,500 feet above sea level. After cycling a mile, he would again note the altitude. Perhaps it would now be 1,850 feet. The difference, 350 feet, was our elevation gain over the mile. David liked to shout out, "That mile was steep. We gained about 350 feet!" I never needed to hear it was steep. My legs told me.

Road signs on mountain passes state the grades in percentages, giving drivers an indication of the road's steepness. David used his numbers to quickly calculate his own percentages, to see if they corroborated those of the road signs. He would take the elevation gain over a mile, divide it by 5,000 feet (a rough estimate of the 5,280 feet in a mile), and shout out the percentage. We learned that as soon as the grade got to be 7 percent, or 350 feet of elevation gain per mile, we had to concentrate on climbing. No more taking in the scenery. Just bear down on the cranks and slowly turn the wheels.

What amazed me about David was he kept a notebook and pencil on top of his handlebar bag while he was climbing so he could record elevation gains. He kept his mind busy doing arithmetic. Once we crested a peak, he gave a summary report: mile one, six percent grade, mile two, five percent grade. Later, we could relive the entire climb, mile by mile.

I had several of my own odometer games. My first was to select a tree, a signpost, or a section of guardrail ahead and guess the distance in tenths of a mile. As I pedaled upward, I kept my eyes glued to the odometer. Upon reaching the destination, if I had been correct on the mileage, I rewarded myself with my favorite snack, a Fig Newton. I also played the reverse of this game. I called it the "don't look" game. I would select something ahead and cycle toward it without referencing the odometer, instead trying to guess the mileage or the time it would take to get there. Simple games, yes, but they made climbing time go by faster.

As we slowly moved up McKenzie Pass, late spring wildflowers bloomed in abundance. I felt like a student in a botany class. With each thousand foot change in elevation, new varieties appeared. We played another game as we ascended the pass: Who could find a yet unseen species of wildflower.

On the steeper sections, the road had long switchbacks, traveling more horizontally than vertically. Back and forth, we rode along the switchbacks, slowly snaking our way up the pass. The temperature was dropping, but we were sweating and the cooler air was refreshing. We were thankful there was no traffic to impede our slow, steady climb.

At one rest break, David took advantage of the absence of traffic by napping in the middle of the bright, sun-warmed road. There he fell asleep, his helmet for a pillow, on the black asphalt.

As we neared the top of the pass, we were surprised to find large lava fields, the remains from erupted volcanoes. The angular, gray-brown lava boulders stretched for miles, in vivid contrast to the glistening beauty of the snowy, sun-drenched peaks in the distance. We had never seen anything like the summit of McKenzie Pass except in photos of the moon. There was little evidence of life, animal or plant. Occasionally, there would be a small plant that had found a small bit of earth to settle into, but that was all. The area was so barren we thought the volcanoes had erupted recently. We were surprised to learn from a description

of the area on our cycling map that these eruptions had occurred more than 400 years ago.

We took photos of each other at the summit to commemorate the climb. Shivering in the wintry air, we donned our cold-weather gear for the descent into Sisters and to the arid, desert region of Oregon known as the Columbia Plateau.

Our four-hour ascent of McKenzie Pass was over. My anxiety over the climb was for nothing. The climb hadn't been difficult, just long. We were eager to start our descent. We still had miles to go.

As I returned to my bicycle, something Day-Glo yellow in the distance caught my eye. Anything of color stood out against the monotonous, rock-strewn background. We rode closer. There, erected amongst the rocks, was a small tent, and next to it was a shiny red bicycle with a yellow covered child carrier in tow. Here was some evidence of life among the boulders! In moments, from behind a large rock, a brightly attired cyclist appeared. He was not accompanied by a child. As we questioned the lone cyclist, we learned he lived in Sisters and made an annual pilgrimage to the summit of McKenzie Pass before the road opened to cars, to celebrate the coming of summer. The young father had left his son behind, instead using his carrier for beer and supplies. From his terse responses we could tell he wasn't seeking conversation. He was on the pass for solitude, and we were interrupting that solitude. So we cycled away, leaving him alone among the rocks.

As we were about to start our descent, David and I had to make our usual decision: Who cycles first? David, stronger and weighing 50 pounds more than I, should roll faster down a hill, but we discovered years ago that I can always overtake him as we coast down a hill. We've tried to figure it out. David is sure he knows why. I have a very small head. How many adults wear an extra-small helmet? My shoulders are narrow, and my backside is quite wide. As I lean over my bike in an aerodynamic position, my body offers little resistance to the onrushing air. I cut right through it, building up speed. (David refers to me as his Cycling Bullet.) David's body is the reverse of mine: large head, broad shoulders, narrow hips—a wide frame offering resistance to the wind. If he goes first on a downhill, I have to wait a few seconds before I start my descent. This time David opted to go first, and I shivered at the top until it was my turn to go.

For the first several miles, high banks of windblown snow lined the road. It was an exhilarating downhill ride as we took curves as wide as we wanted, with no worry about oncoming traffic. I felt like a skier racing down a slalom course. With each 1000-foot drop in elevation, the temperature rose. By the time we reached the bottom, the air had warmed so much we were stripping off layers of clothing. As we rolled into Sisters, loose fitting T-shirts were all we needed.

Was it extreme hunger that made us rate the cheeseburgers we ate in Sisters as the best we've ever had? Or was it the greasy french fries that accompanied the burgers? Maybe it was the fresh lemonade that washed down all those calories. Whatever the reason, it was a memorable eating experience.

As we devoured the burgers, we were pleased we were *almost* to our destination, Redmond. And that we had *almost* completed our toughest day to date: 113 miles and 5600 feet of vertical climbing. But *almost* didn't put us at our destination. We still had 20 miles to go.

We both were pleased about getting over McKenzie Pass, our first climbing challenge of the trip. Now our bodies told us it was time to stop. But we couldn't listen to our bodies. Our day wasn't over. It was an effort to return to the bikes. As my leg muscles went back to work, I made my mind focus on the warm bath I would be soaking in once we got to Redmond.

Whenever we struggled to cycle the last section of road, David would count down the miles to our destination, starting from ten miles out. He was the cheerleader. The first five miles he would shout out the mileage remaining and the last five he would signal with his left hand, throwing his fingers in the air and hollering, "Five...four...three... two...one." Later, when we looked back on the long, difficult day, we never remembered it as being difficult. But as we were fighting to accomplish those last few miles, the day seemed impossible.

June 19

This was supposed to be an "easy day." We had seventy miles to ride and no long hills to climb. But, this was the day we learned the lesson, "*THERE ARE NO EASY DAYS.*" After our long day crossing the Cascades, we slept late. Didn't we deserve it? It was close to eleven o'clock before we started cycling.

The tire David had purchased in Eugene was not of good quality, resulting in repeated flats. By the time we reached Prineville, forty-three miles from Redmond, we had replaced four inner tubes. We couldn't continue changing tubes at this rate. It was already after two in the

afternoon. While having lunch in Prineville, we decided I needed a
reliable tire, as we would be cycling into a remote section of Oregon.
We inquired of residents, looked in the Yellow Pages, and soon learned
the only bike shop in town had gone out of business several months earlier.

Now what? Must I cycle on with the defective tire? We knew
that wasn't a good idea. Returning to the Yellow Pages, we discovered
there were several bike shops in Bend, Oregon, fifty miles away. We
called Hutch's Cyclery, and they carried the Continental cross-country
tire we were seeking. We explained our dilemma—we were touring
cyclists stuck in Prineville without a car.

"Not a problem," said our salesman, Cody. "I'll deliver the tire
to you after work. I get off work at six and will be there around seven.
Where are you staying?"

We located a motel and settled in, waiting for our rescuer to
knock on the door. Shortly after seven, we opened the door to welcome
Cody, a tall young man dressed in plaid shirt and jeans. He looked
more like a cowboy than a bike mechanic. Whatever his look, he was
our savior. Hung over one arm was the tire we needed. We kept telling
Cody how grateful we were for his delivery service, but he shrugged it
off. "No problem. I didn't have anything to do tonight anyway. Besides,
I know how desperate you feel. I've done some touring myself." As
Cody disappeared down the hall, David and I gave each other a "high
five". We had successfully solved our first dilemma, thanks to Cody.
We weren't sure whether it was Western hospitality that made Cody
offer to deliver our tire or that he was a fellow cyclist, but we owed him
a lot. If it were not for him, we couldn't have continued our journey.

We learned a valuable lesson from our unplanned stay in Prineville:
from then on, we had to start early. It made no difference whether the
planned mileage was short or long. Obstacles could suddenly appear.
Terrain could be hillier than expected. Mechanical problems could
arise. We needed time to cope with the unexpected.

While in Prineville, trying to solve our mechanical problem, I
took some time to look around. What was it about the town?

Something was strange. On the way into town we had seen three disheveled young people with two dogs, leashed with clothesline rope. One of the young men was lying on the side of the road as his compatriots tried to thumb a ride. I was riding ahead of David and the prone figure escaped his view. As David veered to avoid hitting the young man, he said, "Sorry about that. You having a slow day?"

The reclining body gazed up, nodded, smiled, and slowly said through a three-day-old beard, "Yeah, man, every day is a slow day!"

Most people walking the main street of Prineville were unkempt. Their jeans had more holes than fabric, their ankle-length dresses were shapeless, and their Birkenstock sandals were worn. Tie-dyed shirts were everywhere. There was enough long, soiled hair in town to keep a barber busy for life. Then I saw the old school bus. Welded on top was the upper half of an old VW bug and the entire creation was painted in psychedelic fashion, with swirls of red, yellow, and orange. I thought I was in the midst of a '60s love fest. We questioned a saleswoman in the drugstore about the appearance of the town's inhabitants. "Oh, that's just people from the Rainbow Festival. They're gathering at a campsite outside Prineville for the week," she casually explained. "The festival is an annual gathering for leftover hippies and young converts to their '60s lifestyle." For festival week, they made Prineville colorful.

June 20

It was cold, very cold, when we awoke. The thermometer attached to David's handlebar bag registered 33 degrees Fahrenheit! We dug out our cold weather gear. We discovered years ago that layering clothes is the key to staying warm. Our first layer was a polypropylene long sleeved shirt and I, bothered by the cold, added a second one—a zippered turtleneck. Next was a polypropylene vest and finally a waterproof jacket. Over our knee-length biking shorts, we wore thick polypropylene tights. If it was very cold, we would top these with loose-fitting rain pants. On our hands we put long-fingered cycling gloves, but for this day I pulled out my cycling mittens. I opened two packages of mini hand-warmers—the type that once the packaging is opened exposing them to the air, they remain warm for hours—and inserted them in my mittens. I wanted to put some mini-heaters in my biking shoes, but they wouldn't fit. Under our helmets we wore wide poly-propylene headbands, and we covered our biking shoes with zippered waterproof booties, made of rubberized fabric, that offered protection from the wind and rain, but didn't do much for the cold. We never found a solution for keeping our feet warm.

Cumbersome in our many layers, we started out. Soon we started climbing, and our bodies warmed up. At the summit of Ochoco Pass (elevation 4,720 feet) in Ochoco National Forest, we spoke with the caretaker of a campground. He described the hard frost the area had overnight and how many campers had complained of the cold, which was unusual for so late in June.

After descending the pass we coasted into the town of Mitchell. The highway sign announcing entry to the town listed the population as 200. Would it be large enough to support a restaurant? We needed breakfast!

Several motorcycles and a camper parked in front of a small, tidy cabin indicated it was a rest stop. As we entered the Blueberry Muffin Café, the aromas of bacon, sausage and coffee filled the air. Ah, we could get breakfast. As we devoured our food, we read a glowing newspaper review of the café that was framed and posted on the wall. We learned Mitchell was a popular breakfast destination. Although the town could not sustain a restaurant on its own, the route we traveled was popular with tourists. The John Day Fossil Beds are close by. The ride through the beautiful Ochoco National Forest draws Sunday drivers. On weekends, the Blueberry Muffin Café is standing room only.

A bubbly, blonde teenager waited on us. She was very excited. "I can't wait to get off work!"

"Why?" I questioned.

"My Mom and I are going to town, and I'm getting my nails done," she replied.

Having just cycled the previous 45 miles with no indication of a town, I asked, "What town are you going to?"

"Bend."

Bend was 92 miles away! So, we learned traveling great distances for services is a way of life for the people living in these remote Oregon towns.

David and I discussed how this contrasted with the rural towns of our native New England. Those towns, settled in earlier times when horses were the only means of transportation, were closer together. You'd never find towns 90 miles apart. Automobiles made the difference.

As the young waitress cleared our table, I asked, "With so few people how does the town run a school system?"

"Oh, we get students from large cities who like our small class sizes to come here for school. We have dorms for them," she replied.

"How many students do you have?"

"About seventy, I think," she said. And to let us know how progressive the school system is, she added, "And we use the Internet for everything."

I wanted to question her further but she waved us off, "Gotta go! I'm off to Bend."

It was an exhausting trip into John Day. Knowing we were doing a day and a half's worth of cycling in one day didn't help me mentally. By mid-afternoon I was ready for the day to be over. We rode rough surfaces through construction sites, where the dust generated from earth-moving equipment clogged our eyes and noses. Highway workers stopped us to flag oncoming traffic through, further slowing our travel. I longed to be on an organized bike trip where a sag wagon follows the cyclists, ready to pick up those having difficulty. If a sag wagon had come by and offered to rescue me from cycling the last 30 miles, I would have been on board in seconds. Each turn of the crank was becoming more difficult. I focused on things other than cycling. I knew my energy level was low. I knew I hadn't eaten enough. Finally, I bonked!

"Bonking" is a cyclist's term for a complete loss of energy. Tears are the only things I have energy for when I bonk. Every movement of your body becomes difficult. To avoid bonking, it is necessary to eat on a regular basis. I had been drinking too much Gatorade, giving me the feeling of being full. I needed to eat more solid food.

We took a rest stop. I forced myself to eat some energy bars. I didn't want to move. I talked to myself, "You can't quit now."

David became my cheerleader. "Melissa, I know you can do it. Ride close behind me and draft. I'll do all the pulling."

Drafting is when the second cyclist of a duo rides several inches behind the first, his body offering resistance to the wind. The second cyclist, nestled in the wake of the first, gets a free ride, *almost*. Turning the cranks becomes easier, except on the hills. Drafting takes concentration. The first rider has to realize that whatever move he makes, someone inches behind will do the same. And the second cyclist has to concentrate on keeping just several inches between bikes. I accepted David's offer to draft.

For the last miles into John Day, I concentrated on David's rear wheel so I wouldn't think about my aching body. I was shaking from exhaustion as we rode into John Day. When we got to our motel I had to sit on the edge of a planter for several minutes to regain enough strength to get to our room. It had been a very tough day for me.

All I wanted to do was sleep. David convinced me to eat and then to go to the motel's Jacuzzi. As I half-slept in the warm, swirling water, I thought about the day after next—our first layover day. No cycling. What a sweet thought! I've found a good night's sleep is the panacea for a physically, mentally drained cyclist. That night I planned to get one.

June 21

Refreshed, David and I set out for Baker City. In the morning we crossed three peaks in the Blue Mountains: Dixie, Tipton, and Sumpter, all with summits over 5,000 feet. Then we relaxed with a long run into Baker City.

We were awed by the space and solitude that defines eastern Oregon. One sign we passed read "No Hunting for the Next 11 Miles, Property of Tri-Creek Ranch." Here was a ranch that extended along the road for 11 miles! We thought of our native New England where many towns don't have a boundary that runs 11 miles. The silence was broken only by the ever-present rush of water, either running down mountains in streams or being electrically pumped into irrigation systems.

From observing the vehicles that passed us on the road, we learned if you want to live in eastern Oregon, you need to own a truck—probably, a double-cab truck. The pickup truck is the family vehicle, the farm vehicle, and the recreational vehicle. We saw trucks that had kids and dogs in the open-air back. Others hauled wood or hay. Another carried a rowboat filled with large inner tubes, all securely tied to the truck. I started identifying with these trucks because I, too, had a truck bed—my B.O.B. carrier. Like the trucks of Oregon, it was multipurpose. B.O.B. carried our dirty clothes to the Laundromat. It hauled beer when we weren't sure we could get it at the end of the day. Newspapers with the sports scores David needed to see were slipped into B.O.B. But there was a downside to B.O.B. It allowed me to carry too much gear. After a week of hauling excess weight over the mountains, I relented and started to lighten my load. I had to admit that David was correct. "Weight is weight, no matter how you carry it."

David had laughed at me when I added the hardback version of Steven Ambrose's *Undaunted Courage*, the story of Meriwether Lewis and William Clark as they sought water passage to the Pacific Ocean, to my gear. I told him I wanted to read a book that had historical relevance as we cycled the country. Its weight was not going to be a problem. It was the first thing I eliminated. I didn't have time to read a book. Whatever spare time I had I used to compose e-mail for my Internet audience.

When your bicycle is your only form of transportation, you protect it. To secure our bikes we both carried heavy chains with combination locks. It was not necessary. For the duration of the trip our bikes never spent a night outside. Whenever we stopped for the day, our first task was to take care of our bikes. It was not uncommon to see us roll our bikes into elevators, to be brought to our room. If we could not take them into the room, we asked for inside storage. Our bikes spent the night in barns, in sheds, in cellars, in coat closets and in vacant conference rooms. We had no need for our heavy chain locks. We left them behind.

I carefully assessed the clothing I brought. Did I really need two "nice" outfits? No! And three pairs of shorts and tops? No! Dressy shoes, casual shoes and sneakers? No... no...no. I found a box and started packing. By the time I finished, the duffel in B.O.B. was significantly lighter. When the sizable package arrived home, our daughter Rebecca, who was living there, laughed, "Only Mom could do this." When I spoke to her by phone to see if the package arrived, she said, "Did you leave yourself any clothes?" I assured her I did.

David also trimmed his belongings, but not to the extent I did. He was better packed than I from the outset. As he looked over his gear, he realized it wasn't necessary for both of us to carry bicycle pumps. He sent his home. We both carried battery-powered night-lights, knowing we might need them for early morning starts or for days that ended late. The handlebar-mounted lights provided us with long-distance illumination, but they were heavy, requiring six size D batteries. The forward frame-mounted water cage held the battery pack. We now reasoned that a single lamp could provide enough light for both of us, as long as we rode close together, allowing one of us to eliminate some weight. I sent my light home and left the six size D batteries behind.

The B.O.B. carrier has a bright yellow warning flag attached to the rear with the letters B.O.B. emblazoned on it. At the time we took the trip, we didn't know what the letters B.O.B. stood for, so David supplied his own definition: "Babe on a Bike." (Later we learned it stands for Beast of Burden.) However, David was pleased that his companion, his "Babe on a Bike," became educated quickly (it only took a week) and reduced her load to the essentials.

June 22

We spent our first day off the bikes in Baker City where we rented a car (no easy feat—we could not locate a rental agency so we called a car dealer). We wanted to see Hell's Canyon. Promotional brochures state that Hell's Canyon is deeper than the Grand Canyon. The relentless Snake River has been forming Hell's Canyon for millennia, creating spectacular cliffs that drop down to the raging river. Large dams have formed huge lakes along the river. We took a jetboat tour to see more of the canyon. According to our boat operator, the Snake River was at a record high for late spring. At the Hell's Canyon Dam the spillway was open, and massive amounts of water thundered to the river below. As we sat safely in the jetboat, we could feel the fury of the cascading water. The noise was so loud we could not hear one another. A continuous spray of frigid water chilled us.

The rapids below the dam were at Class V, preventing all but a few highly skilled rafters from making the challenging trip down the Snake River.

In Baker City we dined at a wonderful old hotel, the Geyser Grand. It was under renovation and had partially opened in May. The builders were attempting to keep it as close to the original Victorian design as possible. We spent the evening in their Palm Court restaurant, with its stained-glass ceiling and dark paneled walls.

Over dinner we discussed our first week on the road. We were pleased my knee was holding up well. Each morning during the first hour I could hear it clicking (something the doctor told me was normal), and then it settled down for a day of constant turning. We talked about our mishaps—the blowout in Eugene and our rescue by Cody in Prineville. We thought of our first week as a shakedown, getting all systems working for the remaining eight weeks on the road. As we discussed our journey across Oregon, we felt we had made a good start. Both of us were holding up well, mentally and physically.

We sipped our coffee and looked up at the hotel's second floor. The guest rooms lined a balcony that overlooked the dining room. Each had an old-fashioned transom above the door, opened to allow a flow of air into the room. The ornate stained-glass ceiling above the dining room allowed light to enter the core of the building. In that restored early 20th century setting, we kept expecting to see a gentleman with a handlebar mustache, a great stogie in his mouth, enter the dining room to meet with colleagues. Over dinner, they would make a deal in lumber or precious metals. Spending an evening in this historical atmosphere was a pleasant way to end the first segment of our cross-country trip.

Chapter 2
Rivers of Idaho

Baker City, Oregon, to		Miles	Elevation Gain (ft.)
June 23	Cambridge, Idaho	111	5,520
June 24	Riggins, Idaho	69	2,830
June 25	Kooskia, Idaho	100	3,830
June 26	Lolo Hot Springs, Montana	98	4,290
June 27	Missoula, Montana	39	240
June 28	Missoula		Layover day
MILEAGE: 417 / ELEVATION GAIN: 16,710 FEET			

Kooskia
Missoula
Lolo Hot Springs
MONTANA
Baker City
Riggins
Cambridge
IDAHO

Total Mileage To Date: 1,040
Total Elevation Gain To Date: 42,070 feet

June 23

At 5:30 A.M., we departed Baker City. As we mounted our bikes, we glanced behind us. The Blue Mountains were aglow in a vibrant pink hue that almost pulsated. It was spectacular. At that hour there was no traffic, so we took our eyes off the road to catch glimpses of the mountains as they changed from a deep pink to a light rose. As soon as the sun broke the horizon, poof! The pink-drenched mountains were gone, returning to their evergreen hue. No longer did I question why Claude Monet painted the same scene at different times of day. Quality of light changes everything.

The Oregon Trail passed close to Baker City, and a museum in town, which we didn't have time to visit, honors that fact. An informative, interpretive site sponsored by the National Park Service sits on a hill outside Baker City, overlooking the old trail. We stopped to view the historic site. David and I left the interpretive center with a greater appreciation of those long-ago settlers who traveled more than 2,000 miles to get to the West. We felt a kinship with them. Their trail master had them up at 4:30, just as David had us. They were on the road by 5:15 and their day wasn't done until they arrived at a predetermined destination, just like the two of us. And like those settlers, we learned to live with just the basics. As the Oregon Trail pilgrims moved west, they continued to unload their possessions. Chairs, china, dishes, beds— all were found lying by the trail, too heavy to carry to the west. And we, too, had pared down our belongings.

It was a gentle downhill grade from Baker City to Brownlee Dam on the Snake River, the dividing line between Oregon and Idaho. A 20 knot tailwind enhanced the sloping grade. It was a cyclist's dream. We flew! At the Snake River we turned south, and the strong westerly winds became a crosswind. We struggled to keep our bikes upright and breathed a sigh of relief when we cycled below hills that blocked the wind.

Just as the wind could be our friend or foe, so it was with the terrain. We learned to read the land. Rivers and streams are the strongest indicators of what type of terrain to expect. If we rode with the river's current, we could expect a downhill slope. If we rode against the current, the slope was a gradual uphill. If there were no streams, most likely there would be hills to climb. Railroad tracks were a positive sign. Rail beds cannot be set at more than a two percent grade, a comfortable one for cyclists.

After a week of cycling, our butts were broken in. We no longer resisted returning to the bicycle saddle each day. However, we still had some bodily pain, in our feet and hands. As a day wore on, our feet,

under constant pressure during hill climbing, and our hands, always
supporting our weight no matter how many handlebar positions we
found, would go numb and then ache. It was not unusual for me to
unclip a shoe on a downhill run and shake some feeling back into my
foot. The same was true with my hands. As I balanced the bike with
one hand, I'd shake the other hand at my side. At rest stops we quickly
removed our shoes and gloves so we could massage our feet and hands,
getting circulation to return. We discovered the best way to revive our
swollen, cramped, sweaty, tired feet and hands was to find a cold stream
in which to dangle them. It felt wonderful. Back at the summit of
McKenzie Pass, we'd dug a hole in the snow and buried our feet for as
long as we could tolerate the cold. It was our peak foot-revival experience.

We knew from previous experience our hands and feet might
cause us problems. We remembered hearing about a father-daughter
cycling duo who had to quit a cross-country trip because their hands
were too sore to continue. To prevent these problems, we purchased
socks that had heavy padding in the ball of the foot and biking gloves

that had extra thickness in
the heel of the hand. Even
with those precautions our
hands and feet remained
our tender spots.

Each afternoon we
searched the roadside for
streams so we could soak
our feet. When we found
one our spirits soared, just
knowing we could luxuriate in the cold water and get some relief for
our aching feet.

Another indulgence of ours was napping. After lunch, wanting
to boost our energy for the remainder of the day, we would take a brief
snooze. David was an expert at finding shady spots. Lying in the shadow

of a towering tree, we would gaze up at the sky. With memories of childhood, we'd point at passing clouds. "Do you see a lion's head in that one?" I asked.

"No, but I see a giant sunflower." David replied. Before long we were in a deep sleep. Wisely, David set his alarm before each nap.

As we cycled into Cambridge, Idaho, we noticed a gentleman waving to us from across the street. It took us a few seconds to realize this was our welcome from Mr. Jack Croly, owner of Hunters Inn. In 1991, Jack, a retired businessman, bought the inn. He told us the inn was once a brothel. It was apparent Jack liked decorating his bed-and-breakfast in an eclectic way. Parked in front was a long white stretch Chrysler limousine, vintage 1958. Jack informed us the limo was in tip-top shape and was used regularly to pick up guests at the Boise airport. As we entered the main house, we saw Jack's collection of Western gear: hanging black bear coats, soiled ten-gallon hats, and distressed cowboy boots. He handcrafted all the furniture. He made tables and chairs from sections of large trees, the usable surfaces sanded smooth and polyurethaned to a high gloss. We complimented Jack on the rugged Western decor he created.

The three of us sat sharing beers and conversation around a tree table. Jack is a native Idahoan and prides himself on his knowledge of some of Idaho's "characters." He told us about the local woman who has been a recluse for decades, fending for herself in the backwoods. She recently was required by the Cambridge authorities to get a phone because it was getting too difficult to check on her in person.

We had our own story to tell about what we thought was an Idaho recluse. On our way to Cambridge, as we cycled close to the top of a hill, a large billboard, made of rough timber, stood on the side of the road. Its message, in vivid red paint, read, "NO TRESPASSING! THIS MEANS YOU! JOE MULLINS OR JOHN PARSONS, IF YOU STEP ONTO MY PROPERTY I WILL **KILL** YOU!" We wanted to stop and take a picture of the sign, but we figured someone who felt that way about trespassers might not take kindly to photographers. As we descended the hill, another sign, the same size with the same message, warned the traffic from the other direction. It made us feel uneasy. We figured the occupant of the property had binoculars, and perhaps a firearm, trained on us.

After our home-style dinner in Cambridge, we stopped at a bar for a drink. I ordered some wine. The bartender said she remembered seeing some around, but wasn't sure she could find it. After a lengthy unsuccessful search of her walk-in refrigerator and the shelves behind the bar, she offered me a shot and a beer. We were in cowboy country, where the drink of choice is a shot with a beer chaser. I'd always thought a shot was whiskey, but the cowboys I observed drank a shot of Bailey's Irish Cream or some sweet liqueur before chasing it down with beer. I know John Wayne would never have had a Bailey's before his beer! I refused the bartender's offer of a shot and a beer and settled for just a beer.

June 24

It was a relatively short ride from Cambridge to Riggins, Idaho. At our lunch break we took the time to chat with our waitress. She told us her husband worked for the Forest Service and was an avid hunter. Each year he tried to kill a cougar and a bear. When I inquired what they did with the dead animals, she seemed surprised. After she skinned and gutted the animals, she explained, she sold the skins. She and her husband ate the meat. From the cougar she made sausage, using only the back meat, because the remainder was too tough. As for the bear, they ate it all. The liver was especially tasty. Although I had difficulty relating to this couple's acquisition and preparation of the meat in their diet, I was impressed by it. Whatever meat I put on our table I purchase cut and cellophane-wrapped from our local market.

As we continued our trip into Riggins, we were again reminded of the toughness and individuality of Idaho women. That January there had been heavy rains throughout Idaho and Montana, resulting in severe mud-slides. Some roads were still closed, and others were under major repair. We spent several hours negotiating our way through a construction site. Heavy equipment—scrapers, bulldozers, large trucks—were everywhere. When we looked more closely at the drivers of the heavy equipment, we discovered many of them were women. There appears to be no glass ceiling in the Idaho construction business!

As we cycled Idaho, we saw pieces of old farm machinery sitting in fields, displayed in front yards, or congregating in farm equipment junkyards. The old tractors looked like Rube Goldberg devices, with cranks, pulleys, chains, valves, and whistles combined in a way that you couldn't imagine how they ever operated. The people of Idaho are resourceful and find various uses for the old equipment. In Council, Idaho, two large tractors dominate the town park—tractors as public sculpture. Individuals use various pieces of equipment as lawn ornaments. Some are creative enough to use the old equipment as planters. In one yard we saw a tractor whose seat was filled with red geraniums, accented with white alyssum.

We arrived in Riggins by early afternoon. Getting those extra hours off the bike was a luxury. I usually spent the time napping and writing in my journal. David read and studied his maps, reviewing the next section of our route. He also compiled "the numbers" of our trip to date. He would test me. "Melissa, what has been our steepest climb?" Or, "On what day did we achieve our fastest miles-per-hour average?" While I tried to record what we experienced as we cycled the country, David recorded our abilities as cyclists.

After a short nap I spent the afternoon sitting next to the Little Salmon, a narrow river with steeply sloped sides, writing. The water in the river was moving too rapidly for me to dangle my feet. I felt I would have been swept away if I attempted the ritual. The color of the water, a muddy brown, carried soil from higher altitudes. It was further evidence of the hard winter. In late June, the snowmelt continued to have an effect on the river's flow.

Our eating habits changed during the trip. As we perused a dinner menu, if we saw it included steak, no matter how it was prepared, we ordered it. Neither David nor I could explain it, but biking long distances caused us to crave beef. At home I seldom put beef on our table, but now we both ate large amounts of it. For lunch we usually had a burger—preferably one with a thick slice of cheese oozing over the top. Dinner was again beef. The closest we could come to explain our craving for red meat was our bodies required some protein or amino acid that beef contained.

We found no gourmet restaurants on our route across Idaho. Our meals were for sustenance only. The most memorable meal we had in Idaho was outside of Riggins, where we ate in the local grocery, hardware, fishing, hunting, and café establishment. Whatever we ordered from the menu was retrieved from the frozen food section of the grocery store and thawed in the microwave. Most eating establishments prided themselves on their pies. Never have we seen so many kinds of pie— peach, marionberry, boysenberry, double chocolate, and strawberry-rhubarb. We figured our bodies needed calories and we enjoyed sampling many of the varieties offered.

June 25

When we left Riggins, we cycled along the Little Salmon River. The sun had just risen. Why were hundreds of trucks and campers lining the sides of the road? My urban mentality wondered where they could be carpooling to in Idaho. Traffic did not seem to be a problem. When we checked the banks of the Little Salmon River, we got our answer. Fishing! All the parked trucks and campers belonged to anglers. At home, we spend our early morning hours getting fit at the neighborhood health club; Idahoans fish.

We were amazed at the diversity of scenery we'd seen in the short time we'd been cycling. Raging rivers, heavily forested mountains, arid deserts, fertile valleys, and hills devoid of vegetation—all had been part of our experience. Often when we crested a mountain, what appeared in the next valley was a totally different landscape than the one we climbed out of. The most pronounced difference we experienced

was climbing White Bird Hill, on our way to Kooskia. On the western side cattle ranches dominate. On the eastern side is Camas Prairie, a fertile valley covered with crops. Colorful fields of wheat, rapeseed and canola extend for miles. At a rest stop we spoke with a farmer who told us the fertile soil is the result of long-ago volcanic activity. The farmer continued proudly that Camas Prairie has the highest per-acre yield of wheat in the country.

Before biking to our destination, the Looking Glass Inn located several miles outside of Kooskia, we stopped to purchase breakfast supplies. We knew we would be on the road early the next day. We also picked up a celebratory six-pack of beer. Carrying bulky items was not a problem with the B.O.B., which was becoming an important part of our cycling team.

When I made the reservation in January for our stay at the Looking Glass Inn, I was told dinner would be available. Walking back into town was not an option. When we arrived at the Inn, tired and thirsty, no one was there. Our knocks on the door and shouts into the yard brought no response. Finally, we tried the door. It was open, so we proceeded inside. A note sat on the table.

Dear Nortons, Please help yourself to drinks in the refrigerator. Am picking up daughter at airport. Back later. Marge

What was later? Panic set in. Were we going to go without dinner? That prospect terrified us, so we opened some beers, munched on some cheese and crackers, and did a search of the pantry to see if there was anything we could cook up for ourselves. As the evening wore on and no one appeared, we felt awkward, but we went to the room assigned to us, showered, and came back to make our own dinner. It amazed us how spaghetti and bottled sauce, with some bread and butter on the side, could taste so wonderful. Compared to nothing, it was a feast.

The owners did not arrive until after we had gone to bed, but when we arose at 5:00 A.M., they were already up preparing a sumptuous breakfast for us. They'd forgotten our dinner request and felt terrible about it. They hoped a special breakfast would make amends.

June 26

We left Kooskia to cycle along the Lochsa River, which brought us to Lolo Pass, the dividing line between Idaho and Montana. The uphill grade was moderate for the first 85 miles. It was a wonderful ride along the Lochsa. I was inspired by the churning rapids of the river, the cool, moist air, and the backdrop of steep, evergreen-covered hills. I felt I was cycling into an Idaho postcard. At one point I stopped and watched a group of rafters being hurled down the  Lochsa. "Hey, want to join us?" one of the rafters shouted. It looked so inviting. Reluctantly I answered, "Sorry, not today."

Farther up the river I saw some single rafters maneuvering their catamarans from a seat perched above the two pontoons. The groups in large rubber rafts seemed to be having more fun. Their screams of delight as they caught white water and got the inevitable soaking were audible long before I saw them.

As we cycled along the Lochsa River, David fell behind. We didn't always cycle together, but we never got too far apart. At every junction we would wait for each other. Along the Lochsa, each wait for David got longer. I knew something was wrong.

"Why are you so slow? Do you feel all right?" I asked him at one stop.

"I'm okay. My legs are just tired."

At the next junction I waited a long time for David to appear. "You don't feel well, do you?"

"Melissa, I'm OK. Just tired." It was a typical male response. Always strong, never showing signs of weakness.

I felt his forehead and knew he had a fever. "David, you are more than just tired. You have a fever."

"Don't worry, I'll make it. I'll just take it slow. I think I might be getting a case of cellulitus." David has had several bouts of cellulitus, where an infection enters the body through a cut in the skin. His doctor prescribed antibiotics that he should take at the first sign of an infection.

"Have you taken some of your antibiotics?" I asked.

"No, I forgot them."

That surprised me. David, the meticulous planner, had forgotten something as important as his antibiotics. My first reaction was to scold him for being so careless, but as we learned early on, it does no good to complain. Instead I sympathized with him and rallied to his side.

"Do you think you can make it through Lolo Pass?" I asked.

"It will be slow, but I think I can do it."

The uphill grade continued, and at mile 85 we got the knockout punch: six miles at a six percent grade. For David it was tough. We took lots of breaks so he could gather up his strength for another section of the pass, but for David it was slow and painful. We were two very happy cyclists when we reached the top of Lolo Pass late in the day. We felt it was a well-earned descent to our destination, the Lolo Hot Springs Resort in Montana.

While I inspected the hot springs Lewis and Clark had described in their journals, David fell into a deep sleep on our king-size bed. I quickly returned, too worried about David to enjoy a soaking in the warm springs. When I got back to the room I discovered David hadn't even bothered to shower before he dropped into slumber. I woke him and convinced him to shower and to join me for dinner. David ate little, forcing down whatever food he could. All he wanted to do was sleep.

June 27

Despite a good night's sleep David awoke with little energy. He didn't want to eat. My suggestion to have me cycle into Missoula and return with a rental car was rejected. He insisted he could get into Missoula on his own. I didn't argue with him. I knew the road to Missoula was well traveled, so if David got into trouble, I could flag down a car or use our cell phone to call for help. With confidence David said, "Don't worry, Melissa. The trip to Missoula is all downhill!" Fortunately, he was correct and we accomplished the 39 miles with ease, reaching Missoula by mid-morning.

Our first stop was a hospital emergency room. After examining David, the doctor diagnosed and prescribed antibiotics for a case of cellulitis, relating it to a cut on David's leg. We left the hospital, drugs in hand, knowing David had a day and a half to recover from his infection. If this bout of cellulitus was like the others, he would rebound quickly once on medication. With rest David knew we could return to our itinerary as planned.

In Missoula, home to the University of Montana and Adventure Cycling (publisher of our cross-country maps), we stayed at Goldsmith's Bed and Breakfast. With David needing to rest, we put aside our plans to visit the headquarters of Adventure Cycling. Our room had a porch overlooking the Clark Fork River and a bike path that paralleled the riverbank. We spent the afternoon watching cyclists, inline skaters, and joggers pass by. David took short naps while I read and wrote postcards. It felt good to be off the bikes, relaxing in the riverside setting.

June 28

During our pre-trip planning, we planned to have our bikes tuned up at every other layover stop. (In assessing our skills, we realized that neither of us is mechanically minded.) Although our bicycles were running well, it was time for our first maintenance stop. Nothing more than lubrication was needed. As the trip progressed, however, we learned our scheduled maintenance stops were a wise decision.

Missoula is popular with cyclists. The surrounding area is filled with trails for mountain bikers and many cross-country cyclists pass through Missoula on their treks to either coast. So when we told our bike mechanic about our trans-America ride, he wasn't surprised or impressed. He related how last week he worked on bicycles for a group of men who were also doing a coast-to-coast trip.

On the recommendation of our mechanic, we booked dinner at Shadow's Keep, a restaurant high on a hill overlooking Missoula. The castle-like structure with a wraparound porch was the perfect setting to watch the late evening sunset and view the five valleys that converge in Missoula. As we lingered over dinner, we talked about how lucky we were. If David had to get ill, he had done so when we were close to a city. What if David had taken ill in some remote area? What would we have done? Hitchhiked? Used our cell phone for emergency help? We put those thoughts aside and enjoyed a spectacular Montana sunset.

Across the street from Goldsmith's B & B was a large sports bar. It was the weekend of the Big Fight: Mike Tyson vs. Evander Holyfield. All tickets for viewing the fight in the sports bar had been sold. The noise from the crowd as patrons cheered on their favorites in the pre-liminary fights could be heard at Goldsmith's. As time for the headline fight approached, we wandered over. We stood chatting with the bouncer at the backdoor of the bar. Soon, he invited us in at no charge, as long as we didn't obstruct anyone's view. With more than thirty TV monitors, that would be no problem. The crowd in the bar was already into the upcoming fight. Shouts of "Tyson!" and "Holyfield!" echoed throughout the smoke-filled bar. We joined in. When the third round brought the fight-ending ear bites by Tyson, we shouted, "Vampire!" Some people in the crowd picked up on that! It was a lively scene, with patrons shouting in disbelief. "Vampire!" "The fix is on!" "I want my money back!" "Bring me another beer!" We settled for another beer and a final look at the disappointed patrons, still searching for the fight of the decade.

Chapter 3

Big Sky Country

Missoula, Montana, to		Miles	Elevation Gain (ft.)
June 29	Sula, Montana	94	2,930
June 30	Dillon, Montana	100	5,060
July 1	Virginia City, Montana	57	1,480
July 2	W. Yellowstone, Montana	86	4,250
July 3	Cooke City, Montana	90	5,500
July 4	Cody, Wyoming	77	5,340
July 5	Cody		Layover day

MILEAGE: 504 / ELEVATION GAIN: 24,560 FEET

Total Mileage To Date: 1,544
Total Elevation Gain To Date: 66,630 feet

June 29

As we departed Missoula, we encountered our first rain. It was a heavy
rain that kept up until mid-afternoon. Our cycling jackets were waterproof
for a while, but then they got soaked through and acted like wetsuits,
keeping us warm as long as we pedaled. Waterproofing our gear, however, was a problem. Large garbage bags, layered two and three thick,
worked well for a time, but then water started to seep in. We never
found a solution for keeping our gear completely dry.

Neither of us minded cycling in the rain, but water on the road
slowed us. It was after 7:00 P.M. when we arrived at our destination,
the Lost Trail Resort, half way up the Lost Trail Pass, south of Sula,

Montana. The hot springs the resort offered were tempting, but food and sleep were more important. We rushed to clean up and get to dinner. Our tired muscles needed food more than they needed a soak in the hot springs. We knew we needed energy because the next day we had to complete our trek up Lost Trail Pass and then follow it with Chief Joseph Pass, peaking at 7,214 feet.

Our host at the Lost Trail Resort, when hearing of our plans to ride to Dillon the next day, tried to dissuade us. "It's a hundred miles to Dillon and you'll have more hills after you get through these two passes."

We told him we knew what lay ahead—it was a section of road we'd ridden before. During the morning hours we would cycle through Big Hole Valley, one of our favorite places from a previous bike trip. We recalled the snowcapped Bitterroot Mountains lining the valley, the miles of split-rail fencing, and the awkward looking beaver slides— large wooden structures that catapult hay into towering mounds. We wanted to stop in Jackson, a town in the middle of the valley, to see if the talkative bartender still worked at the luncheon café. More importantly, was he still rooting for the Boston Red Sox?

June 30

We awoke at 5:00 A.M. to continue our assault on the Lost Trail Pass. The temperature was in the low thirties, with a cold mist descending the pass. We welcomed the six percent grade; cycling hard was a way to keep ourselves warm.

On our way up the pass, I discovered that my odometer was not waterproof. The rain of the previous day had caused moisture to collect in the mechanism, and it stopped. I felt I had lost a friend. Spending long hours alone on a bike, my odometer was my faithful companion. It recorded my daily distance, current speed, and most importantly, total distance. It allowed me to play distance games that took my mind off hill climbing. What upset me most was now no more miles would be recorded. I wanted verification in the form of an odometer readout that I was doing this bike trip—every mile of it! I shook the odometer. I reset the battery. Nothing worked. I set it aside, disappointed. By the next day the odometer had dried out and started to work again. I reset it so it agreed with David's and renewed my friendship with my handlebar computer.

At mile six we crested the Lost Trail Pass, turned east, and continued the next mile to the summit of Chief Joseph Pass, where we crossed the Continental Divide. We didn't linger at the summit. It was too cold. We quickly put on our cold-weather gear as we prepared for our descent into Big Hole Valley. Our hands and feet were particularly susceptible to the damp cold. It was a difficult decision for us: Should we go fast in the descent and be cold or should we slow down, hoping we could stay warmer? We chose to speed it up and get to a breakfast spot as soon as possible. By the time we stopped in Wisdom, at the upper end of Big Hole Valley, we could no longer feel our hands and feet. No sooner did the waitress take our order than David and I retired to our respective restrooms. We kept the electronic hand-dryers running and tried to warm our hands and heads. Our biking shoes and socks also spent time under the warm jets of air.

Although we felt prepared to cycle in all weather, we've learned there are some conditions in which you cannot make yourself comfortable. Although we layered with polypropylene garments so the sweat our exercising produced would wick away from our bodies and evaporate, the weather was too cold and damp to achieve comfort. Our hands and feet remained cold. We discovered it was particular to cycling— the trunk of your body could be sweating from exertion yet your appendages felt frozen to the bike. Years ago, we learned putting our feet directly into plastic freezer bags, underneath our socks, at least kept our feet dry on days when moisture penetrated everything. For this trip we even carried latex gloves that we wore under our full-fingered cycling gloves on damp, cold days.

For the remainder of the day, Mother Nature gave us a full kaleidoscope of weather conditions. As we cycled the length of Big Hole Valley, the rain came down in sheets, hampering our vision. We never saw the Big Hole Valley we fondly remembered. Instead, we kept wiping our glasses with the back of a gloved hand to rid them of moisture just so we could see the road in front of us. In Jackson, we discovered our Red Sox fan had moved on. The skies cleared briefly for our climb out of the valley, and we stripped down to T-shirts. At the summit we returned to our long-sleeved shirts and jackets for the long descent. During the afternoon we watched dark clouds move across the hilly terrain. In the distance a towering cumulonimbus cloud, its anvil top stretching outward, produced a circle of heavy rain accompanied by lightning crackling across the sky. We picked up the pace, not wanting to ride in the severe weather we saw advancing. As we got nearer to Dillon small hailstones bounced off of us. The winds picked up. Lightening bolts and rumbling thunder were closing in. We cycled faster.

On the outskirts of Dillon, I saw an advertisement painted on the side of a building for an inn that offered fine dining and comfortable rooms. We were drawn to it like magnets. The motel in which we had planned to stay was located several miles on the other side of town and we didn't think we could pedal another mile. We pulled up in front of the Centennial Inn. I rushed in and rang the bell on the reception desk. In moments we heard quick steps from a back room and a cheery, plump woman greeted us. "Hello, may I help you?"

"Do you have a room?" I asked in a pleading voice.

"Yes, I've got a room," replied the smiling innkeeper, her kitchen apron still on and her hands pushing back strands of graying hair that had fallen into her face. Seeing our biking attire, she continued, "You're lucky. That is bad weather coming our way."

In the room next to the reception hall, we saw a dozen set tables. "Can we get dinner?" David asked.

"Of course. What time do you want to eat?" asked the innkeeper.

"How about seven?"

"See you then."

We unloaded our gear and went to our room. As soon as we closed the door behind us, we exchanged a high five and a resounding "Yes!" What a wonderful change of plans! We didn't care if the skies opened up or if hail fell or if winds blew; we were safely inside.

I rushed to the bathroom and filled the footed porcelain tub with hot water. I needed a long soak to take the weariness out of my body. David, seldom one to soak in a tub, waited in line. He, too, wanted to relax in a warm bath to help erase the difficulty of the day.

At dinner we discussed our luck in finding the Centennial Inn. The food was plentiful and tasty. Our room was warm and spacious. Our wet clothes were renewed by the complimentary use of the inn's washer and dryer. For the two of us, weary and wet from a long day of cycling, it was heaven.

Our room at the Centennial Inn had a unique feature: twin beds that were the highest we had ever seen. You couldn't flop onto them. You needed to step onto a side rail and then swing yourself up onto the mattress. It was an odd feeling to be reclining with your body closer to the ceiling than to the floor. However, we had no trouble sleeping on those elevated beds.

Our stop at the Centennial Inn was only the second time we did not adhere to our itinerary. We made Dillon, our destination, but we stayed someplace else. Our first deviation was back in Oregon when we had problems with my tire. But this time our deviation caused my family some concern. Unknown to us, my sister Cynthia's two sons, Chris and Brian, who were driving across the country to their home in Washington, waited for us at our planned stop, a motel on the other side of town. As the winds howled and hail fell, our nephews called their mother.

"Hey, when did you last talk to Uncle Dave and Aunt Melissa? Are they still doing their trip? If they made it to Dillon I hope they are inside because the weather here is terrible."

"Last I heard they're still cycling," replied my sister. "They probably stopped short of Dillon to avoid the weather. Don't worry about them."

We never got that surprise visit from our nephews, but we did beat the storm into Dillon.

July 1

The next morning as we prepared for our ride to Virginia City, a Centennial Inn guest wearing a Western style shirt with well-worn jeans and holding a steaming cup of coffee wandered over.

"I saw the two of you on the road yesterday. I felt for you. "

"Are you a cyclist?" I asked.

"Yup. I ride back home in Texas. I bike with a group on weekends. We each take turns driving a sag. Who drives support for you?" he asked.

At this, we smiled. "No one. We carry everything," replied David.

Support was what we gave each other every day.

I supported David by letting him be the sole navigator. I never argued with him about which roads to take. He created the route, and whatever decisions he made, I accepted. I never complained when he made a routing error. David offered me his support by cycling close to me as I slowly ascended long hills. He put his superior climbing skills in check during this trip. We were doing this adventure together. We were a cycling team!

We also decided early on that whining was out. On a trip such as ours, wherein we had to get to our planned destination each and every day, our mental outlook had to be positive. Each day we had to mount our bikes and ride—no complaining! We found laughter to be an instant boost to our spirits. We chuckled whenever we donned our rain gear. How could we not laugh as we saw the tops of plastic bags peeking out from our black stretch booties? Our fluorescent yellow jackets, the hoods tied down securely with a bow beneath our chins, prompted additional giggles. Visored hats stuck out from beneath our hoods. Opaque wraparound glasses covered our eyes. From our appearance, we could have been visitors from outer space. What we laughed about the most were the inquisitive glances we received from people as we peeled off our rain gear. Occasionally someone would ask, "Hey, why do you have plastic bags on your feet?" Apparently, not many people considered plastic bags a form of waterproof protection.

Shortly after leaving Dillon we passed Beaverhead Rock. The large outcropping was the landmark Lewis and Clark's young Shoshone guide, Sacagawea, recognized from her youth. Throughout much of this trip, we crossed sections traveled by Lewis and Clark. Lolo Pass, Lost Trail Pass, and Beaverhead Rock all had historical markers commemorating their inclusion in the travels of Lewis and Clark. We occasionally joked that the explorers purposely stopped at these places so future vacationers would have historical markers at which to stop and learn about their adventure.

After two long cycling days, we were pleased our ride into Virginia City, Montana was going to be short and relatively flat. With the luxury of spare time, we talked with some locals at both a morning break and at lunch. It was interesting to hear how the ranchers in nearby Twin Bridges, Montana view the world—a life very different from the ranch life depicted on the television show *Bonanza*. The independent rancher, owner of his own spread, is becoming a thing of the past. Only big corporate conglomerates can make ranching profitable. We spoke at length to one rancher who said that although he had more than a thousand head of cattle, he and his two sons were barely making a profit. They would probably end up like their neighbors, selling their ranch to wealthy individuals for recreational use, getting more money for the land than they could by ranching it. At lunch, the café owner told us having outsiders come in and buy up the land had created another problem—the privatization of the rivers. Traditionally, the rivers have been open to all for fishing. But with rivers passing through private property, some questions had arisen as to who gets to use them. According to the café owner, it was going to take a bill in the state legislature to protect the public's use of the rivers.

We arrived in Virginia City early in the afternoon. A large number of summer tourists walked along the main street of the restored mining town, visiting shops—the dry-goods, the blacksmith and the ubiquitous saloon. A small playhouse offering a variety of melodramas from years gone by is popular with tourists. In winter, the population drops significantly. However, Virginia City is a functioning city, serving as the county seat and has a large, prominent courthouse located at one end of the restored main street.

As soon as we were shown to our room in the charming guesthouse, the Wilbur Fiske Saunders, we collapsed into bed to get the sleep we'd

missed the past two days. After awakening, we joined our innkeeper, Eva, on the side porch where we rocked in a swing while chatting with her. She informed us that Wilbur Fiske Saunders was one of the leading prosecutors during the tumultuous mining era when Virginia City was overrun by criminals and vigilantes. After 1889, when Montana became a state, he became one of the Big Sky Country's senators.

July 2

David and I like dogs. Any dog will do. Seldom can we pass one without petting it. As we quietly left the Wilbur Fiske Saunders House at the break of dawn, a rambunctious but friendly golden retriever greeted us. We both jumped off our bikes to give the affectionate dog some tummy rubs and scratches behind the ears. Big mistake! Our now devoted golden retriever decided she needed an early morning run, so she joined us as we started the long climb out of Virginia City. As soon as the first car sped down the hill, we knew we were in trouble: Our canine friend chased cars. And she was serious about it. No shrinking violet. Her ears perked up at the sound of a vehicle, and as soon as it got close, she attacked, full speed ahead. We watched her do this just once. After that, each time we heard a car, David or I jumped off our bike and grabbed her. We wanted to be spared the horror of seeing her crushed before our eyes. Keeping our retriever friend safe slowed our progress. She kept our eyes and ears busy looking and listening for traffic. As we approached the summit, our furry friend showed no signs of leaving our side. It was obvious the dog wanted the adventure her new cycling friends offered. We hailed a passing car and asked the driver, a young woman, to drop the dog off back in Virginia City. It was a struggle to get the dog in the car. No sooner did we get her onto the backseat than she jumped out the driver's door. The young woman was kind and very patient. By the time the three of us got the dog secured in the car, all of us had mementos of our canine friend: mud from her wet, soiled coat was spattered all over us.

At the top of the hill, clouds surrounded us. We cautiously started our descent through the thick layer of moisture into the sportsmen's town of Ennis. It was an exhilarating ride—coasting down the hill, breaking free of the clouds, picking up speed, and seeing the Madison River Valley below, basking in early morning sunlight.

After breakfast, we cycled up the Madison River Valley, accompanied by a traffic jam of fishermen pulling boats. Each angler was filled with the hope of catching his limit of trout.

It was late in the afternoon when we reached our destination, West Yellowstone.

July 3

Hoping to beat the traffic, we were on the road at sunrise to start our ride through Yellowstone National Park. At that early hour we were surprised to see long lines of cars and RVs waiting at the entrance to gain admission to the park. There was no way to beat the traffic on that summer day. Most of the roads in the park were in poor condition. We figured they were built by government employees during the Great Depression and since then maintained only with patchwork. Most drivers were going slowly, negotiating the bumpy roads and looking at wildlife and scenery, and they gave us whatever space we needed.

For long stretches through the park, we rode past forests that had been destroyed by the great wildfires of 1988. We stopped at several roadside turnouts to get a more complete view of the devastation. It was a slow process, getting the charred, dead lodgepole pines to drop to the ground. The blackened standing tree trunks that stretched on for as far as you could see were a stark contrast to the newly sprouted bright green of young pine that covered the ground. We marveled at Mother Nature's work, with the end of life and the creation of life so vividly displayed in one expansive view.

In the afternoon we climbed Dunraven Pass. The summit was covered with snow, deep in some places. We stopped and watched youngsters enjoy a summertime fling. Parents ducked as their children hurled hastily made snowballs. Family laughter echoed throughout the summit snowfields.

On our descent we entered an area of Yellowstone we had never visited, the Lamar Valley. As we coasted down the pass we saw alpine meadows covered with a rainbow of wildflowers—lupine, daisies, sweet pea. Stately snowcapped peaks ringed the valley. Each mountaintop glistened in the early afternoon sun, framed by a brilliant blue sky. Falls below the snowline spewed torrents of water to the valley below. Soft, spring-green grasses, awakening from their winter dormancy, covered the valley floor. Roadside streams churned, overflowing with snowmelt, echoing the sound of tumbling water throughout the valley. The air smelled of newness, of Mother Nature beginning her seasonal cycle. It was a feast for the senses.

Descending Dunraven Pass was dangerous. The road was filled with large potholes and a steady stream of traffic was negotiating the Pass. We stopped at one bend in the road so we could look at the valley below unimpeded. A middle-aged couple—he French, she an American—approached us. "We would love to be cycling, but with this traffic, we were afraid to try it. Aren't you nervous?"

"We just ride and let the traffic look out for us. This road is so bad the traffic has to go slowly," replied David.

As the four of us gazed out over the valley, the Frenchman exclaimed, a lovely Parisian accent to his perfect English, "I've never seen a more beautiful sight!" We agreed. We thought the beauty of Lamar Valley on that summer day so special, we vowed to return, in spite of the bad roads and heavy traffic.

Late in the afternoon, as we started our climb out of Lamar Valley, we saw a roadside turnout filled with tourists, all of them focusing binoculars on a distant mountain. Curious, we stopped.

"What are you looking at?" I asked a young man, his back to me.

Without dropping his binoculars, he said, "A big grizzly. He's moving across the top."

No one turned to speak to us. They didn't want to lose their sighting of the fearsome creature. We tried to locate the bear with our naked eyes, but we were unsuccessful. We moved on.

Cooke City, outside the northeast entrance to Yellowstone National Park, was our day's destination. Both of us were charmed by the small town, with a population of only ninety in the winter. We learned it takes a hardy soul to survive in Cooke City during the winter. The main pass into Cooke City, the scenic Beartooth Highway, is closed from November to May. The large amount of snow the area receives and the steep grades along the Beartooth Highway prevent plows from keeping the road clear. In winter, the only access to Cooke City is through the park, using the Gardiner, Montana entrance, a distance of almost 50 miles. More than 50 feet of annual snowfall is normal for Cooke City, and all who live in the town snowboard, ski, or snowmobile. There are no lifts for skiers; they hike up, or persuade a snowmobiler to take them to the peaks. A waiter told us the postmistress and her husband celebrate the 4th of July by taking their snowmobiles up to the high country for their last ride of the season. Finding snow would not be a problem this year; there was plenty of it surrounding Cooke City, at an altitude of 8,000 feet.

July 4

As we pedaled our way across the United States, we saw lots of wildlife. Deer were the most common, but we also saw moose, elk, and a golden eagle. For automobile drivers traveling at a much greater speed, sighting a large animal was a special event. They would park by the side of the road and pull out their cameras. I have a vivid recollection of one of these drivers.

We left Cooke City to climb for several miles, and then we had a long descent. I was riding ahead of David on the downhill, when a passing motorist on the opposite side of the road tooted his horn to get my attention. I cautiously gazed over, and the driver was frantically waving his arm out the open window. I put on my brakes and came to a stop. My heart was pounding. I could feel it beating in my head. Why would someone wave a cyclist down on a clear, smooth descent?

There had to be something dangerous ahead. Was it the most feared of all animals, a grizzly bear? The driver put the car in reverse and came alongside me. I was breathing hard and fast. My body was shaking. With a big smile on his face, the elderly driver told me there was a mature male moose ahead on the right. He had just taken his picture. I felt both relief and anger: relief at knowing my life was not going to end at the paws of a grizzly bear, but anger at having a wonderful descent interrupted. I managed to smile at the gentleman and thanked him for the information about the moose's location. I did stop to view the moose, but I would have preferred a fast, uninterrupted descent.

Cycling long days, we found it necessary to use energy boosting products. Late in the afternoon, if we were still on the road, we needed a pick-me-up. After testing several different products marketed to athletes, and assessing their energy-boosting powers, we felt we had become experts. We soon developed the Norton Rating System. Our criteria were based on several factors. First, did it taste good? If it didn't pass that test, the product was dropped from our selection. Second, how effective was its energy boosting power? Was it fast-acting? Slow to revive the system? Third, how convenient was it to use? Was the packaging too difficult to open while cycling? Was a stop necessary so the product could be consumed? Our scorecard:

> PowerBars.................................... *Yuck*
> Clif Bars..................................... Tasty, but dry
> GU... Magnifico!

We stopped eating PowerBars because of their poor taste, and although we occasionally ate Clif Bars, we had to have water available to wash them down. GU (pronounced "goo") rated highest with us. The near liquid product comes in small plastic packages and is convenient to carry. We liked the taste of every variety of GU, but we had our favorites. Our ratings:

1. Vanilla bean
2. Orange burst
3. Chocolate

The best attribute of GU was how quickly it acted. It seemed to be just minutes after consuming the frosting-like gel that there was more spring in our legs, and correspondingly our spirits picked up with our renewed energy. Most afternoons one of us would shout out, "GU time", just as beer drinkers might shout out, "Miller Time!" David would then pull up beside me and offer me a packet of GU from his handlebar bag selection.

With our teeth we would tear open the three-inch packets and suck out the sweet jelly-like contents. No dryness. No need for water. Just great taste, sliding over our taste buds, giving our bodies a needed boost.

We tried to replenish our supply of GU at each layover. When it was not available, our disappointment was visible to the salespeople. Nothing ever compared to GU!

On our way across the West, we met several touring cyclists—most of them single men. We always stopped to chat and compare itineraries. Most cyclists had trips planned that were not as long as ours—work and family commitments prevented them from being on the road for longer periods. All were envious of us. We met one man back in Idaho who was in his seventies and was traveling from Oregon to Virginia. We rode with him for a while. He said he had retired to Tucson, Arizona, so that every day he could indulge his love of cycling. Each summer he got on the road for a trip and this was going to be his longest. We asked him if he got lonely. "No," he replied. "I'm in no hurry so I sometimes stay in a campground for a day or two. I meet other cyclists and ride with them for a while."

Another of the lone cyclists we encountered was a young man from Denver. When we questioned him about his solitary trip, he grinned as he showed us his cellular phone. "I don't need to have a companion when friends and family can be reached at any time," he explained. We also carried a cellular phone, but our purpose was not to reach friends and family on a daily basis; we wanted it on hand for emergencies. David and I agreed that touring alone would not be as much fun. We needed each other's company to share sights, travails, conversation and laughter.

On this trip, David and I were enriched by each other's personalities. Statistician David has always been one to measure things. He measures how far he runs. He times himself, mile after mile. He sets up statistics about average speeds over given lengths of time. He records wind speeds. His attention to measurement detail is recorded in notebooks he keeps by his bedside. If he needs to know how fast or how far he ran on May 12, 1994, he can give the precise answer. Did he lift weights on June 8, 1995? That, too, would be included in his exercise notebook. His recording of various aspects of the trip provided us with our initial dinner conversation. David would bring his bike-trip notebook to dinner and compile the daily statistics. We discussed distance, elevation gain, time on the road, wind speed, whether we'd had a dreaded headwind or a cherished tailwind. We compared the ease or difficulty of biking days. For David, the trip was an athletic adventure to be recorded for future reference. He needed numerical verification of his endurance and fitness. I, too, looked forward to the daily compilation of the numbers. It was gratifying to discuss them when I knew I'd accomplished a difficult ride.

David sees his world through numbers, patterns, and the relationships between them. I see my world visually. Throughout the trip, my eyes were constantly scanning, looking for a scene of beauty that I could draw David's attention to or I could describe to my Web page audience. David would have missed many memorable landscapes without my roving eyes. I got him to stop and look at a golden, haying field surrounded by aging split-rail fences nestled below majestic, snowcapped mountains. I made him slow down to see a hillside covered with pink and purple lupine. One morning I hollered at him to stop. Jumping over a fence nearby was a group of deer. One of the males had a new downy-soft seasonal rack.

David was the trip's photographer, but I was the one looking for scenes worth shooting. Early one morning, we spent half an hour trying to capture a photo I thought would be beautiful. In the low angle of the sun, our biking shadows formed elongated, elegant figures in the golden glow of a hayfield. We took turns—one of us cycled by, while the other tried to photograph just the shadow. We were sure we had an award-winning photo, but when we saw our results, we were disappointed. Our lack of photographic experience was evident. However, we still have a memory of those lovely shimmering shadows racing across the field.

There is a downside to my looking around as I cycle. Between us, we have had about a dozen biking accidents. One was David's, and the rest were mine. Focusing on the countryside, I wouldn't know he'd slowed down or stopped, and I would ride into his rear wheel. Fortunately, most of the accidents resulted more in embarrassment than injury. Over the years I've learned to keep a safe distance and to give myself enough road space so I can react to David's changes of pace. For his part, David has learned to give me a hand signal before he slows down or stops.

During the week of July 4th in Billings, Montana, there was a large convention for owners of Honda Gold Wing motorcycles. Throughout Montana and Wyoming, we saw hundreds of these large, well-appointed motorcycles on their way to Billings. Each bike we saw was polished to such a high gloss, we could see our reflections in their hubcaps. We never knew motorcycles came with so many amenities: padded leather saddles that seemed to contour the owner's backside;

small trailers that matched the motorcycle's color scheme; matching helmets that included headsets so the driver and passenger could converse. Many of the bikes carried a colorful stuffed animal, tied securely to the rear seat with a bungee cord. We didn't know if that was something peculiar to Gold Wing riders. As the bikers motored by, we heard their expensive speakers pumping music into the countryside. Although our bicycles were humble forms of transportation next to their expensive pieces of machinery, the motorcyclists thought of us as "brothers of the road." They all waved and gave us the thumbs up sign. We shared something: like them, we travel on two wheels, put up with the elements, and love adventure.

As important as a well-conditioned body is to cycling long distances, a well-conditioned mind is more important. Even though we learned the lesson "There Are No Easy Days" back in Oregon, and even though this got us on the road early each day, we discovered our expectations also played a role. When we looked at a day's proposed ride and discovered the mileage was low, we couldn't help it—we mentally relaxed. We anticipated the day ending early, allowing for some extra time off the bikes. By David's pre-trip calculations, our journey from Cooke City, Montana to Cody, Wyoming was going to be 53 miles. Not a long day! By noon, we planned to be sipping margaritas at an outdoor café, watching the people of Cody celebrate the 4th of July. Our first indication that it was not going to be an easy day was a mileage sign stating Cody was 63 miles away. Wait a minute! Wasn't Cody just 53 miles from Cooke City? At first David thought the road sign was a mistake. Later as we passed the 53-mile marker on our odometers, we knew we were in for a tough one. No longer was I looking at the beautiful landscape. I was feeling every turn of the crank, not because I was in danger of bonking, but because I no longer wanted to be cycling. We weren't certain of how far Cody was, so our minds couldn't even calculate an arrival time. We hadn't reached Cody by mid-afternoon. Instead we climbed Dead Indian Pass, a steep six-mile ascent. The praise we received from the tourists at the summit did not ease our down moods. We wanted to be in Cody. The day dragged on. The hills seemed steeper. The temperature felt hotter than that registered. It was a difficult day for both of us. We knew the cause. We expected something easier than what we got. Our minds were not prepared for this assault on our endurance. Finally, when our odometers registered 77 miles, we rode into Cody. When David compiled his numbers, we realized we had completed the hilliest day of the trip thus far, climbing 5,340 feet in 77 miles. A tired, disgruntled pair of cyclists, we claimed our room at the Irma, the centrally located hotel in Cody named after Buffalo Bill's daughter.

It had been a day that seemed endless, and we were thankful the next day was a layover day. No early alarm. No biking. Instead, it was a day of relaxing and seeing the sights of Cody. As we sleepily ate our dinner, we discussed how the trip was one-third complete. We also talked about how making this trip together had changed something in our relationship, even after 32 years together. We developed a new closeness, a better sense of each other's needs, a deeper respect for each other's individuality. What had caused it? In retrospect, we think it came from working together toward a common goal. David and I were a team, putting aside petty daily distractions that normally would have caused some disharmony, to achieve that goal.

July 5

Cody is a city that plays up its cowboy image and its famous namesake, Buffalo Bill Cody. The city was created in 1895 by a group of businessmen who asked legendary scout and showman Buffalo Bill if they could name the town after him. As we looked around, we saw Cody was filled with real cowboys and wanna-be cowboys. Only the brand of jeans a real cowboy wears gives it away. Wrangler jeans are for real cowboys. All others—Levis, Ralph Lauren, or Calvin Klein—are for the wanna-be cowboys. A cowboy's boots and hat were also a giveaway. If there was no dirt on the boots and no sweat stains on the hat, he was not a working cowboy. Whether real or wanna-be, most people strolling the streets of Cody were proudly wearing western-style clothing.

The town of Cody takes its Buffalo Bill Cody heritage seriously. It has a museum in Buffalo Bill's honor, and rodeos are offered every night in the summer. Fourteen western-art galleries line the main streets. Cody also has enough boot and saddle makers to make any cowboy or cowgirl happy. Each night during the summer tourist season, a group of players from the Cody Preservation of Western Culture Society stages a gunfight in the street next to the Irma Hotel.

A large crowd gathered to watch the evening shoot-out. At the first volley of gunfire, we shuddered, our ears ringing. My instinct was to call 9-1-1, until I realized the guns were part of the show. By the time the players finished performing their scene, most of the characters were stretched out, dead. Most young members of the audience were screaming in fright. Perhaps this was realism we watched—a true picture of the Wild West.

As we strolled the streets of Cody, we found a gallery named Raven Fine Art that featured contemporary works. As we looked over the collection, a piece of ceramic caught my eye. Posed in a laid-back, relaxed position, a dour-looking hound dog beckoned me. A silver sheriff's badge held a commanding position on his burgundy shirt. On his feet was a pair of glossy black cowboy boots. A large Stetson hat sat firmly upright on his head. He was wonderful. I bent over to read the name of the piece. Incredible! The piece was titled BOB DOG. I knew he was destined to be mine, forever a reminder of our day in Cody, Wyoming and of my trusty cycling friend, the B.O.B carrier. The United Parcel Service guaranteed BOB DOG's safe delivery to our home.

Chapter 4
Cowboys

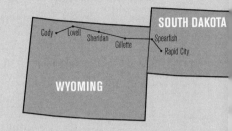

Cody, Wyoming, to		Miles	Elevation Gain (ft.)
July 6	Lovell, Wyoming	49	320
July 7	Sheridan, Wyoming	103	7,230
July 8	Gillette, Wyoming	103	4,410
July 9	Spearfish, South Dakota	97	2,930
July 10	Rapid City, South Dakota	49	1,590
July 11	Rapid City	Layover day	
MILEAGE: 401 / ELEVATION GAIN: 16,480 FEET			

Total Mileage To Date: 1,945
Total Elevation Gain To Date: 83,110 feet

July 6

Our ride out of Cody took us through the Big Horn basin, a stretch of
land beneath the Big Horn mountains. The basin is a hundred miles
wide and a hundred miles long. It's an agricultural area, growing sugar
beets, green beans, corn, and hay. Not far outside Cody we rode by a
large group of dilapidated, green wooden buildings. All of them
appeared abandoned. A fence surrounded the area. We were curious
about the site. Soon, we spotted a roadside marker and stopped. We
learned we were looking at the Heart Mountain Center, the involuntary
home to many Japanese-Americans during World War II. Discovering
the history of the site, our initial feelings were heightened. The place

was indeed eerie. No sign of life—just abandoned, dilapidated buildings nestled in the plains below Heart Mountain. And Heart Mountain itself was unusual. With an immense heart-shaped projectile protruding near the summit and looking as if it just dropped out of the sky, there was no doubt where the camp got its name. Many people believe that gathering up Japanese-Americans during World War II and forcing them into camps was an unfortunate decision of the United States government. As we looked over the site, we felt Heart Mountain Center deserved greater recognition for its part in World War II history. But other than the roadside marker, we saw no commemoration of the internment site.

The trip to Lovell was short, so we took our time, spending the morning stopping to read the historical markers Wyoming has put up along its roadways. We learned about the Mormon presence in the basin and how the Mormon settlers created the canal system that is still in use today. We saw our first oil field, where the bobbing heads of the . oil rigs looked like giant birds seeking food in the ground. As we neared Lovell, we saw fields that contained the oddest-looking piece of farm machinery we'd ever seen. The structure was the size of a road-building dump truck, but it had no distinct shape. Surrounding a core were numerous chutes and conveyor belts, extending out in several directions. It looked to be constructed from pieces of a giant erector-set kit. What impressed us the most was the structure was mobile, with wheels sitting beneath the core. Although many fields contained the unusual looking piece of machinery, we remained perplexed as to its use. Finally we got an answer. At lunch our waitress informed us the equipment harvests sugar beets.

As we cycled the flat Big Horn basin to Lovell, we could see the Big Horn Mountains ahead. They formed a solid ridge of peaks from north to south and dominated the landscape. We had the entire day to view what we had to ride over the next. Edging closer to our challenging ride, we kept telling ourselves, "the Big Horns don't look *that* imposing." We neglected to remind ourselves the mountains were still fifty miles away.

Back in Cody, while we were watching the shoot-out, we chatted with a crop-duster, his speech slurred from too many Fourth of July celebratory beers. He told us that five days a week he takes one of his company's single-engine planes and from about thirty feet above the ground he sprays crops. We were impressed by his piloting skill. "Oh, it's nothing. You get used to flying low. You gotta stay alert, though. The ground can come up on you quickly so you gotta be ready to pull up."

When we described our trip, saying how we planned to bike over the Big Horns, the daredevil pilot couldn't believe it. "Are you two crazy?" Here we thought he was crazy, flying so low to the ground. He made us a sincere offer. "I have tomorrow off. I can drive you over in my truck."

We scoffed at him. We told him how we had cycled many passes in the Colorado Rockies and in northern New England, so we were up to the task.

"But you haven't done the Big Horns!" he replied. He was making us feel apprehensive, but we kept reminding ourselves we were on a cross-country route that was described on the Internet. If other touring cyclists had done it, we felt we could, too.

A habit most cyclists have is to inquire about the terrain of roads ahead. Unless you are lucky enough to ask a fellow cyclist, it is a bad habit. Automobile drivers never give accurate answers. Their responses are not intentionally false. It's just that terrain is something they don't feel as they cruise along, powered by a large engine. As often as we've told ourselves to never, never, never ask an automobile driver about roads, we continued to do so. A Big Horn scouting report we got from one driver said to expect several miles of very steep grades, and then a steady five percent grade to the summit. That sounded doable. We also knew, as a last resort, we could take the advice of our cycling friend, Lee, who always says, "I've never met a hill I couldn't walk."

We arrived in Lovell before noon. We rested during the afternoon and then retired early after dinner. We wanted to be ready for our attack of the Big Horn Mountains. As I lay there sleepless, thinking about the difficult climb ahead, David snored quietly, fully confident the next day's ride was well within our abilities.

July 7

We watched the sunrise as we cycled the first ten miles, a gentle uphill grade away from Big Horn Lake. The closer we got to the mountains, the more arid the landscape became. Off in the distance we sighted a lone deer as it made its way among the scrubby vegetation. Slowly we moved toward those Big Horn peaks that appeared so doable yesterday, from fifty miles away.

Unlike mountains that are heavily forested and hide the road ahead, our day's challenge was laid out for us to see. We watched, as a red pickup truck snaked its way down the steep slope, the road through Medicine Wheel Pass. We put our coping strategies in place. How far did we think it was to the second bend in the road? Two miles? Three miles? David won the first contest. It was three miles. What did we think the grade was from one curve of the switch-back to the next?

Seven percent? Eight percent? Neither of us won that. It was a constant ten percent, with no breaks.

Slowly we made our ascent. We required frequent stops. In the steepest sections we would cycle a mile and take a break. I even used a coping strategy I developed years ago while hiking. On a peak at thirteen thousand feet I was exhausted and ready to quit, thinking I couldn't make the fourteen thousand foot summit. Then I remembered a seasoned climber saying the best way to overcome the lack of oxygen at higher altitudes is to slow down. Take baby-steps. Take one tiny step up, then another, and another. Soon I was hiking to a mantra "baby steps," repeating it over and over as I put one foot in front of the other. It worked then, so I tried it now. A steep mountain was my obstacle, not lack of oxygen. I forced my pedals into the downward stroke in cadence to a steady, low whisper of "baby steps," which I dragged out to four syllables. I never looked up except when I planned to take a break. It would have been too discouraging.

David, forever the statistician, noted that when road signs on other mountain passes had said to expect a seven percent grade, it was five percent or six percent. In the Big Horns, the road signs said to expect ten percent grades, and they were accurate! We knew we were doing something difficult. Every few miles there were turnouts for RVs and trucks to cool their brakes on the descent. There was little traffic. The few trucks we saw were empty, none wanting to haul a load in either direction.

Our frequent breaks allowed us plenty of time to admire the Big Horn Basin behind us. The photos we took of the trip attest to that. We have more pictures from our ascent of the Big Horns than from any other part of the trip.
As we gazed back from 5,000 feet, we felt we were viewing the scene from an airplane. We had climbed that high.

As we crept upward, we met cattle that were being driven up to higher grazing fields. We never got side-by-side with the cows to get a good reading, but we felt they were moving faster than we were. The cattle posed another problem for us—a big problem. The road was covered with cow pies! Climbing that steep hill was difficult enough without adding the slippery coating of cow dung to our tires. Not to mention that our sweet-smelling mountain air had taken on a new aroma. But we laughed it off, chalking it up to another memorable hill-climbing experience.

At noon we thought we made the summit. Usually there are signs to indicate you are at the top, but here we found none. Where was the summit sign? And why was the road continuing down a steep grade, only to ascend again for a lengthy ten percent grade? My legs were shouting, "No more!" But we kept moving. It was one o'clock in the afternoon before we reached the true summit. Sitting in a pile of snow was the summit sign. But it was another sign that caught our attention. It gave a better description of the climb we had just completed. The large sign, which was directed at motorists, read: "Caution. You will drop 3,600 feet in the next 10 miles. Memorize where the brake cooling areas are."

It took us seven hours to get to the true summit. It was a slow, torturous climb, but we did it! We laughed and smiled as we raised a toast to each other with our Gatorade-filled water bottles. We put the Big Horn climb into our memory banks. We knew we would never do it again on a bicycle. It was a one-time-only adventure!

The day should have ended at the summit. We were so happy the brutal climb was over that a natural letdown followed. We didn't want to bicycle any more. Our legs were telling us they had done enough work for one day. But we couldn't listen to our bodies because we still had miles to go to our destination. After putting on our jackets, we returned to our bikes to pedal along the flat summit.

Our perseverance was soon rewarded with the best downhill ride we've ever had. It went on for 16 miles. The road surface was smooth, with no potholes or seams, and we could see forever, out to the plains ahead. We had crossed the last mountain range of the West. When we stopped at the Big Horn Recreational Area Visitor Center to see if we could purchase a memento poster of Medicine Wheel Pass, the courteous woman volunteer asked, "Did you really come through Medicine Wheel on your bikes? "

"We did," David and I responded in unison, proud of our accomplishment.

"But why did you go through Medicine Wheel? The pass south of here is not nearly as steep. We advise RVs not to attempt Medicine Wheel Pass. The grades are just too steep. Just last year an RV with five passengers on board burned out its brakes, and they all lost their lives when the camper crashed through a guardrail. I give you credit for coming through the pass. You two must be strong. And a bit crazy."

We agreed with her.

I hadn't known about the lower pass. When I questioned David about why we didn't cycle the easier pass, he mumbled something about how his route was shorter. He said it was the most direct way from Lovell to our destination, Sheridan. But I didn't need to listen. I knew why we cycled Medicine Wheel Pass. David likes challenges. Today he had one.

In our exhilaration over conquering the Big Horns, I forgot to take my asthma medication, and I paid the price. As we sped along the last 10 miles into Sheridan, my lungs shut down. I knew this was no simple attack. In moments I was off my bike, gasping for air. Quickly I used my inhaler. David returned to my side to calm me. He grabbed his cellular phone to call for help. I didn't want to be rescued, so I asked him to wait a minute. David rubbed my back and talked to me. "Concentrate on breathing slower. Relax, Melissa."

Slowly I returned to a normal pattern of breathing.

David asked, "Can you make it into Sheridan?"

I wanted to try. Those ten miles were the most difficult I have ever cycled. Even the Big Horns were easier. I would give a few turns of the crank and then coast. My lungs were not willing to work beyond a minimum capacity. Our speed, normally about 15 miles an hour on flat terrain, dropped to several miles an hour. David stayed tucked in behind me, telling me to stop whenever I needed to. When I saw the Holiday Inn sign extending high above the highway, I whispered, "At last." We made it into Sheridan unassisted.

Once inside the air-conditioned Holiday Inn my lungs cleared. We both made a mental note to remember to have me take my asthma medication. No more situations like today.

July 8

We left Sheridan expecting to coast along the plains to Gillette, our next stop. Our minds were ready for an easy day. It was not to be. The first disappointment was that we had to cycle on an interstate highway. We never would have chosen to ride an interstate, but in parts of the West there are no other roads to get you from one locale to another. When that is the case, cyclists are allowed on the highway. The Web page itinerary we were on described Interstate 90, from Sheridan to Gillette, as desolate; that is, a cyclist would never know he was on an interstate. Not true. On that summer day Interstate 90 was filled with traffic, most of it trucks and RVs. Only a wide breakdown shoulder kept us cycling. The next disappointment was the terrain. This area may be described as the plains of Wyoming, but we climbed hills cycling those plains. And then there was the heat. Gone were the cool temperatures of the mountains. To round out the day, we had strong crosswinds.

As we neared Gillette we raced thunderstorms. It was thrilling— and a bit frightening—to watch the lightning and the rapidly moving dark clouds in the distance. The desolate plains offered us no coverage other than the ditch beside the road. So we raced the storms. We made a game of it, observing the lightning and starting to count: one-one thousand, two-one thousand, three-one thousand. Six seconds represented a mile's distance from us. As we struggled against a downdraft from a nearby storm, we eyed our hotel. We were happy to be inside when the storm broke.

As David checked into the hotel, I chatted with a coal company executive. He told me Gillette is the largest coal-mining area in the country, with the largest reserves of coal in the United States. The coal is extracted through strip mining, in which the earth is plowed away to reveal the coal that sits close to the surface. The executive assured me strict environmental laws make the mining companies reclaim the land once they ceased mining. As we rode into Gillette, we saw areas we knew must have been reclaimed mining areas, the terrain being too angular to be natural. The next day when we left Gillette, we observed what appeared to be an abandoned strip mine that had not been reclaimed. The open, scarring wounds of the earth were visible, and I wondered if environmental laws covered all sites no matter when they stopped producing. Would this site be reclaimed, or would it remain as a testimony of how destructive strip mining is to the natural landscape?

July 9

The winds continued. Because the temperature was now in the 90s, we did not mind the strong crosswinds; they cooled us. Once we stopped cycling, the heat became penetrating.

We rode the last twenty miles into Spearfish, South Dakota, on newly laid asphalt. The black road surface was soft, and we could see the heat shimmering in the air above the surface. As we checked into our motel, we heard the sound of rushing water. It was only minutes before our shoes were off and we were soaking our feet and hands in Spearfish Creek. Next to satisfying a daylong thirst, having cold water wash over our appendages was an incomparable treat.

As we soaked our feet and sipped a well-deserved beer, we heard laughter and voices. In moments a young couple floated into view, sitting in what appeared to be truck-size inner tubes. They navigated the swift current by bouncing off the sides of the creek. As we watched the cold water wash over them and listened to their laughter fill the air, we could not think of a better way to spend a hot summer evening.

Our dinner in Spearfish was at Sanford's, a funky Cajun restaurant that was opened by some college students. The food was spicy hot, and although we didn't try all 110 beers they had to offer, we sampled more than a few.

July 10

Heat was now our daily companion. We tried to be on the road early, even if the ride was short. We expected our arrival in Rapid City, a layover stop, to be before lunchtime. But along the way we needed to stop in Sturgis to buy some T-shirts for our friends who own Harley-Davidson motorcycles. Every August, Sturgis hosts a huge rally for Harley fans. As we cycled into Sturgis, we saw the annual rally keeps the town occupied year-round. Its streets are lined with motorcycle-equipment and souvenir shops, all offering wares to Harley enthusiasts. Because it was early July, we knew we would ensure our Harley friends back home they would be the first on the block to have official Sturgis rally T-shirts. We purchased the shirts and mailed the gifts from Rapid City.

It was in Sturgis that I had a minor run-in with an automobile driver. Actually, it was a pickup truck driver. The four-lane road that leads into Sturgis has no shoulder, so it was necessary for us to take part of the road. Most drivers kindly gave us the space. While we were waiting at a red light, the pickup truck inched its way next to me, and I kept moving toward the curb to give him the room. Finally the truck was beside me. I was cramped and out of balance between the truck and the high curb. I glared at the driver. I wanted him to meet my gaze so I could do something to show my anger. What would I do? Flip him the finger? Mouth an obscenity? It was probably a good thing the driver's eyes stayed forward and he quickly sped away when the light turned green. A line of tattoos ran along his arm, long blond hair flowed down his back, and his head was wrapped in a bandanna. His truck squealed and shimmied as he sped away. From all indications he probably would not have taken kindly to a cyclist calling him a bad name.

As we traveled across the West, David enjoyed the music. We heard nothing but country music, his favorite. Restaurants, bars, even passing motorcycles with large speakers played country music. When David was not listening to it, he was singing it. His favorite was Willie Nelson's "*On the Road Again*," a perfect traveling song for us. David sang often and he sang well, drawing the attention of passing motorists and the occasional cow.

Trucks were the vehicles of choice in the West. Each truck came with a dog, often two dogs, that rode in the truck bed and were very protective of the vehicle. I learned that the hard way. When I approached a two-dog truck in the parking lot of a restaurant in Lovell, Wyoming, talking softly and offering the canines a pat, the dogs greeted me with deep growls, displaying mouths full of sharp teeth. It was not affection the dogs wanted. They wanted me to know the truck was their property, and I'd better keep my distance.

July 11

In Rapid City we stayed at the Hotel Alex Johnson, built in the 1920s by Alex Johnson to honor the Sioux Nation. Rapid City was the first place we'd traveled where Native Americans are a large part of the population. I am an admirer of Native American crafts, so after inquiring, we went to Prairie Edge, a wonderful gallery dedicated to the crafts of the Plains Indians. I was unfamiliar with the work of the Lakota. Seeing their highly detailed beadwork, both in jewelry and on garments made of animal skins, was enlightening. Unlike the Navajo and Hopi of the Southwest, who create pottery, jewelry, and rugs, the Plains Indians work with beads and use animal skins, bird feathers, and parts of trees to create their art. Exquisitely detailed dresses made of doeskin hung on the walls. When I inquired how most buyers intended to use the dresses, I was told that most were purchased to be hung, as you would a painting. After the release of the movie *Dances with Wolves*, in which Kevin Costner's bride wore an exquisite white beaded dress, some brides were buying them for wedding dresses. I couldn't leave without purchasing an artifact that highlighted the skill of the Lakota. I settled on a doll whose hair is bison fur; her dress, heavily beaded doeskin; and her features, well-crafted beads.

In Rapid City—our layover day locale—we rented a car so we could drive up to Mount Rushmore to view the mammoth sculpture of the four presidents: George Washington, Thomas Jefferson, Abraham Lincoln, and Theodore Roosevelt. We were not prepared to be impressed, expecting a tacky tourist area to surround the site. As we drove up Mt. Rushmore, the massive sculpture loomed over us. We were overcome by its size and how it dominates the surrounding mountains. As we entered the park, we walked beneath beautiful stone archways, which

led to an amphitheater below the mammoth sculpture. Here we took in the surroundings and reflected upon the four United States presidents depicted in granite. The stonework of the archways and amphitheater is also of granite, which adds to the majesty of the Mt. Rushmore site. Rarely does something man-made enhance what nature has created. Here it does.

Like so many visitors to Mt. Rushmore, we questioned why Teddy Roosevelt was one of the presidents chosen for the memorial. Washington, Jefferson, and Lincoln, most people agree, were great political architects of our country. But why Roosevelt? The sculptor, Gutzon Borglum, had been acquainted with Teddy Roosevelt, and he felt Roosevelt, with his need for adventure and his love of the American landscape, embodied the American spirit.

A second side-trip we took from Rapid City was to the infamous town of Deadwood, centered in the Black Hills. Deadwood is the town made famous by Calamity Jane—pony express rider, crack shot, and daredevil— and Wild Bill Hickok—marksman, poker player and victim of a fatal gunshot in 1876. Both graves are in Deadwood's Mount Moriah cemetery. In 1989, with tourism down, Deadwood initiated gambling. With the influx of money, many of the buildings have been restored, and the entire town is on the National Registry of Historic Places. We made early dinner reservations for Jake's, the restaurant associated with Dan and Kevin Costner's casino, Midnight Star.

The building for Jake's and Midnight Star has been restored to magnificent splendor. No detail was overlooked. The building has dark wood-paneled walls polished to a glossy shine, marble-lined bathrooms with brass fixtures, and art that covers the walls. Most of the artwork is centered on films starring Kevin Costner. Costumes from his various movies are framed and hung along the walls and stairways, accompanied by photos and posters advertising Kevin Costner movies.

We felt underdressed as we entered the elegant third-floor restaurant. But as we looked at the diners already seated, we relaxed— casual attire was accepted. When we planned the trip, we knew we would have to pack clothing that was suitable to wear in upscale places such as Jake's. Whenever we were required to "dress up," I found black crepe pants and a slinky black turtleneck acceptable. Not wanting to wear the same thing every time we went to a nice restaurant, I carried two belts; in my mind, that *was* two different outfits. For shoes, I carried low-heeled black mules that stored one within the other. David brought a sports shirt and a pair of khaki pants as his dress-up outfit. We found our selection of clothing suitable for any place we stayed or dined.

As we walked down the few stairs to the main dining area of

Jake's, the sparkling array of glasses and the crisp white linens that adorned the tables were just a prelude to a wonderful dining experience. The extensive menu contained all the necessary items to ensure our dining pleasure. For me, it was a salad of mixed greens. Throughout most of the trip, a salad meant iceberg lettuce covered with heavy dressing. For David—whose definition of an upscale restaurant is one whose menu contains choices you can't understand—it was the inclusion of some items that were so esoterically described he had to ask the waiter for assistance.

After the waiter interpreted the menu for David, we chatted with him. It was early in the evening—and Jake's was just half-full, so he could spare the time. As we discussed where we lived, the tall, angular waiter, his face tan and deeply lined, proudly announced, "I'm a native of the West. My family homesteaded in 1876, and we've been here since."

His response wasn't the first indication we'd had that having one's roots go back to the Homestead Act of 1862 was important to inhabitants of western states. We'd driven by ranches and farms where signs read, "Homesteaded by the Bailey Family since 1882" or "Ranched by the Smith Family since 1873." The Homestead Act of 1862 provided a settler with 160 acres of free government land. Title to the land was presented after five years if the settler had complied with the Act's restrictions: built a house and lived on the property; dug a well; plowed at least ten acres; and fenced in part of the acreage.

Our waiter wanted us to know he was a true westerner and not a transplant. His western roots reached far back to those adventurous people who used the Homestead Act to start a new life.

Before making the difficult choices for our meals, we celebrated our achievement to date with a glass of champagne. Traditionally, in our cycling careers, whenever we accomplished a century (a 100-mile ride), we celebrated with a bottle of champagne. On this trip, the tradition went by the wayside. We did centuries on a regular basis so the celebratory champagne was meaningless. We talked about upping the ante to 125 miles.

Our dinner at Jake's was wonderful. Not wanting it to end, we slowly sipped our wine, lingered over rich, chocolate desserts and coffee, and discussed our return to the road.

After our tasty dinner we went to the first-floor casino to spend the complementary $10 worth of chits we were given at Jake's. We chose to play the quarter slot machines. Neither of us is a gambler. We have never even purchased a lottery ticket. When David had to be shown to push the "cash out" button to get his winnings, he realized that earlier he had walked away from a machine because he thought it was unlucky. The machine displayed 44 credits, but no money had come out. Some lucky gambler followed David on that machine.

Once initiated, we played heartily. When David's machine gave a credit of 500 points, I quickly pushed the "cash out" button. It was a slow process, having 500 coins drop into the metal tray. The loud jingle of quarters, as they were expelled from the machine, drew the attention of the casino patrons. Our naiveté as gamblers was apparent. We later learned we could have asked one of the floor attendants for the winnings and not subjected the casino's patrons to all the noise. We took our $125 worth of winnings, knowing we had beaten the odds, and headed back to Rapid City.

Chapter 5
Good Lands, Badlands

Rapid City, South Dakota, to		Miles	Elevation Gain (ft.)
July 12	Interior, South Dakota	76	900
July 13	Winner, South Dakota	131	4,570
July 14	Pickston, South Dakota	82	1,100
July 15	Yankton, South Dakota	68	1,370
July 16	Sioux City, Iowa	70	470
July 17	Sioux City		Layover day

MILEAGE: 427 / ELEVATION GAIN: 8,410 FEET

Total Mileage To Date: 2,372
Total Elevation Gain To Date: 91,520 feet

July 12

As we packed up our bikes for an early-morning departure from Rapid City, a walker, sipping his coffee, stopped to talk with us. He was intrigued by my B.O.B. carrier. With a long, blond pigtail hanging down his back and his head wrapped in a black leather bandanna, he seemed to me to be a Harley-Davidson fan. When I questioned his allegiance, he immediately went into a diatribe about how all the "fat cats" who thought owning a Harley was cool had ruined the image of motorcyclists. He longed for the days when bikers were carefree individuals who loved their bikes and needed to be on the road. He related how years ago the rally at Sturgis was for camaraderie and talk of bikes, from antiques to the latest models. All participants rode their Harleys to Sturgis. It was not like today when half the attendees at Sturgis don't even ride their bikes, but haul them in a trailer. The depth of his disappointment in what the Sturgis rally had become was evident. He went on at length about how he worked long hours in construction during the summer months so he could take time off during the winter to restore antique Harleys. When he spoke of his restoration work, his eyes took on the look of love. He discussed details we didn't understand, but we could tell just speaking to someone about his work on old motorcycles brought him pleasure. As he examined the B.O.B., he worked in his head how he could construct something similar for his cycles. We bade him good-bye, maneuvered our bicycles onto the road and added another interesting person to our trip collection.

Our ride to Interior, gateway to Badlands National Park, was our best day of cycling since commencing the trip. Every parameter of cycling scored a perfect ten. The road surface was smooth—no seams, potholes or construction areas to impede travel. A wonderful tailwind pushed us along. The traffic was so light we could count on one hand the number of cars we saw. The terrain was flat—very flat.

The temperature was hot, but quite tolerable. And the views were wonderful. Most of the day we looked out on the expansive fields of Buffalo Gap National Grasslands. In the distance we could see the eerie, unique projections of Bad-lands National Park. It was a perfect day! We covered the 78 miles easily, arriving in Interior by lunchtime.

The literature we had read about seeing the surrealistic Badlands area said the best viewing was at sunrise or sunset, when the angled light brought out the coloration of the rocks. We spent the afternoon relaxing by our cozy cabin at Cedar Pass Lodge, which is within the perimeter of the park and is run by the Lakota. We waited for sunset. As evening drew near, a large, ominous cloud from the west approached. We realized a walk in the park would not be a good idea. The downdrafts from the impending storm were so strong we had difficulty making our way to the main lodge for dinner. As we dined, Mother Nature provided us with a light and sound show that rivaled anything we had seen thus far. The lightning, thunder and heavy rain continued long into the night. We felt like children cuddled in our bed, listening to the heavy rain on the roof, knowing we were secure in our little cabin. In the middle of the night, we were abruptly awakened when the comforting whir of the air-conditioner ceased, knocked out by the violent storm. By our pre-dawn start, the skies had cleared and the air-conditioner had snapped back into action.

July 13

Our ride to Winner, South Dakota was scheduled to be the longest of the trip—131 miles by our pre-trip calculations. Both of us worried about it. While David was planning the trip, he called several places in both Interior and Winner to check on the terrain and the road conditions between the two towns. All assured him: The

road from Interior to Winner is flat. It was evidence again we should *never* listen to automobile drivers!

After the previous night's storm, a strong wind from the west set in. For the first thirty miles out of Interior, we headed directly south, fighting the crosswind. The contour of the road was like ribbon candy, not the flat terrain we were expecting, and we thought biking the one hundred thirty one miles would be impossible. We were averaging fewer than ten miles an hour, struggling with both the hills and the crosswinds. After thirty miles our route turned east and the strong westerly winds hit our backs—at more than twenty miles an hour. We flew up and down the rolling terrain! Each time we had to turn off an easterly heading, we struggled to keep our bikes upright. But with the wind at our backs, it was a cyclist's paradise. Who cared about terrain? We wanted to rig sails to our bikes to take greater advantage of the tailwind. When we arrived in Winner, we realized fate had been kind to us. Unbeknownst to us, we had cycled into the next time zone, Central Standard Time, and had lost an hour. We celebrated biking our longest mileage to date in record time with beer and snacks at a Winner sports bar.

The morning part of our ride was across the Sioux reservation, Pine Ridge. As we cycled through the reservation, we kept looking for a place to get provisions. Finally we saw a gas station and convenience store ahead and coasted into the parking lot ready to quench our thirst. A young boy greeted us, curious about why we were biking through the area. As we stepped inside the store, we were greeted by a thin, elderly Sioux woman. What struck us immediately as we looked around was the store's absence of food. All we saw was a cooler with a few sodas in it and a rack containing a dozen candy bars. There was no food that could offer energy to a cyclist. We decided soda and candy were better than nothing. When we inquired about the empty shelves, the woman said she had to go to Rapid City to get provisions for restocking. Most weeks she felt it was better to keep the gas station open for road traffic and not close it so she could leave to get supplies.

We spoke to the shopkeeper, who had been educated off the reservation and had returned to her native land. Her grandson, playing in the parking lot, was in her charge, as was the operation of the gas station and store. We asked her about the large, well-kept ranches we occasionally saw as we biked through the reservation. She informed us those ranches did not belong to the Sioux, but were grandfathered in when land was set aside for the reservation. The ranchers, we were told, paid rent to the Sioux. These ranches stood in sharp contrast to the housing occupied by the Sioux. We would cycle by miles of barren land, seeing only an occasional rundown dwelling. Then suddenly we would see beautiful split-rail fencing. Cattle roamed over the landscape. Erected above a well-cared-for drive would be a hand-carved wooden sign indicating the ranch's name. And then it was over, returning to the barren landscape. The Sioux woman told us that unemployment was very high on the reservation. It was not necessary to tell us that; it was evident everywhere we looked.

An industry that South Dakota has created for itself is pheasant hunting. Winner, South Dakota claims it is the pheasant-hunting capital of the world. Although pheasant is not indigenous, the game birds were brought in and thrive in these environs. According to a bartender we met, fall is a hopping time in the region.

Locals leave, renting their homes to people from around the world. The bartender recalled many Italians being there for the previous year's hunting season.

The sparkling, clean streams and rivers we had seen throughout the West disappeared in South Dakota, replaced by ones filled with silt. The White River, which runs through the Badlands, would be named Latté River if the settlers of the West had known that term—the river is the color of rich, cream-filled coffee. As the homesteaders said when they encountered these streams, "The water is too thick to drink, but too thin to plow."

July 14

In Pickston, South Dakota, we crossed the Missouri River. Lewis and Clark had hoped, falsely, that this river would transport them to the Pacific Ocean and give the United States a coast-to-coast water route. After checking into our motel on the eastern side of the Missouri, we walked back a short distance to Fort Randall Dam. The large lake formed above the dam is filled with clear water, and the numerous bait and tackle shops along the road indicate fishing in the lake must be good. A large hydroelectric plant, with extensive infrastructure, stands on one side of the dam. The river below it is as clear as the lake. A few days later, after we had crossed from South Dakota into Iowa, we saw the Missouri River was no longer clear; it took on the appearance that earned it the nickname "the Big Muddy."

July 15

In Yankton, South Dakota, we stayed in the Mulberry Inn. Our hosts, a middle-age couple, informed us when South Dakota was still a territory, Yankton was the capital. The inn was once the home of Joseph Ward, a prominent minister who rallied support for South Dakota's 1889 statehood. His home has been lovingly maintained over the years, and the couple who run it as a bed-and-breakfast are proud of the historical significance of their property. They told us that Ward, who already has a special place in South Dakota history, has been honored further: He is one of the South Dakotans to be represented in the United States Congress's Statutorium in Washington, D. C., where statues of two worthy "native sons" from each state are displayed.

We were intrigued by the decor of the Mulberry Inn. The entry level had parquet floors combining light and dark woods in an intricate geometric pattern. It was polished to a high gloss and upon entering we immediately removed our biking shoes, allowing only our socks to touch the elegant surface. Floor to ceiling glass windows, their panes glistening in the afternoon sun, were draped in heavy, yellow damask hanging in thick, full folds. In the two sitting areas off the main hallway, floral-patterned area rugs were spread beneath plump, silk-upholstered sofas and chairs. It was not a comfortable setting for sweaty, dirty cyclists. We didn't dare sit in a chair until we had showered off. If we had been told we were looking at rooms that had been featured in *Architectural Digest*, we would not have been surprised.

David observed that in Yankton, if he took a short ride over a bridge spanning the Missouri River, he would be in Nebraska. Our official itinerary did not take us through Nebraska, but David, forever the numbers person, could not resist adding another state to our list. While I took a much-needed nap on our luxurious king-size bed, a ceiling fan blowing cool air over me, David ventured into Nebraska. When he returned to awaken me, he had to boast. "I did it. I went to Nebraska." After that, whenever I called out we had crossed another state line and tallied our total, he reminded me he had a higher count by one.

Along the way whenever we talked to people about our trip, they invariably ended the conversation with "bike safely" or "take care of yourself." We felt fortunate we'd experienced no mishaps. Since the first week when we'd had tire problems, we hadn't even had a flat. There were situations in which we thought about our safety. Biking along interstate highways, which we had to do in Wyoming and South Dakota, was risky. Speed limits ranged from none, for traveling during daylight hours in Montana, to seventy-five miles per hour on the interstates. Vehicles were never more than ten to twenty feet from us, and most were traveling faster than seventy-five miles per hour. The noise from large trucks was deafening, and the draft the trucks created when they passed forced us to hunker over our bikes to maintain stability.

We never took our eyes off the road while on an interstate, because a broken bottle or other piece of debris could have set up a bad situation. Whenever a vehicle came too close to us, we noticed it was usually an RV. We figured that many of the RVs were rented and the drivers were not aware of how wide a vehicle they were driving. We found most drivers to be friendly and courteous. So many occupants of vehicles waved to us, we couldn't wave back to all of them. We started giving a nod of our heads in recognition of their greeting.

At a stop back in Wyoming, a young couple approached us. They told us they had recently moved from Texas and had purchased bicycles. They were doing daily trips around the area and cycling was becoming an enjoyable pastime for them. They were interested in our trip, asking about our daily mileage, how we carried our gear, and what resources we used for creating our itinerary. The young man, after learning how far we had journeyed, inquired, "Have you had any trouble from crazies? Have you been threatened?"

Our response was a surprised, "No!" Being bodily harmed was something neither of us had considered. His inquiries gave us pause.

The man continued, "I would never venture on a trip such as yours without protection. My favorite is a 9mm gun." With that he patted his right front pants pocket, his protection a daily companion.

We didn't question him about the legality of his concealed weapon. We were too stunned by his need for a weapon on a daily basis to inquire.

As we cycled across South Dakota, we noticed many drive-in movie theaters. We thought this type of movie presentation had long since passed into history. Not in South Dakota. What made it amazing was that the eastern part of the state is on the western edge of the Central Time Zone, so during the summer it doesn't get dark until after 10 P.M. Most theaters we passed were offering a double feature. They had the first movie at ten, the second at midnight, and got you home after 2 A.M.

South Dakota is farmland! Fields of wheat and corn stretch to the horizon. One particularly beautiful view was from the top of a low rise. Stretched out in the valley ahead was a gigantic patchwork quilt of golds and greens. Roadside cornflowers offered a touch of blue. The gold was the winter wheat, ready to be harvested. Large coils of hay lay everywhere: in fields, along roads, even under high-tension wires. All land was used. Farm equipment dealers, their salesrooms lining the road into Winner, South Dakota, displayed machinery of every type. Local radio stations announced current grain prices, and banks had signs that continually updated the beef, hog, and corn prices instead of the Dow Jones.

Cattle, which we saw frequently, were curious about two people on bicycles. If we spoke to them, they often would move off into the pasture. It became a game of ours. Could we get the cattle to move, upon hearing our voices? "Giddy-up there, dogies." "Good morning, Bossie." Half the time the cattle would move. They sauntered away, only occasionally moving at a run.

On our way into Winner, we passed a wild game ranch. A herd of bison was in the pasture. These were the first bison we'd seen on the trip, wild or domestic, and it was the first bison calves we'd ever seen. We stopped to take a picture. As we were setting up the camera, a truck stopped and the driver called us over. He warned us that if the bison did not like what we were doing, they could easily  break through the fence to get to us. When we returned to our picture taking, the herd started moving and so did we, cycling as fast as we could away from the fence.

Living in South Dakota means you have to contend with severe weather. As we rode along an interstate highway, we observed that all the entrances to the highway had large gates that could be closed, shutting down the highway. Snow fences, ten to twelve feet high, lined the highways. The past winter had seen such a heavy snowfall that many ranchers in the Dakotas lost a significant number of cattle. We read in a local newspaper about a grassroots program initiated by a rancher to get cattle farmers from other states to donate a cow or two to the damaged South Dakota herds. Only Angus and Hereford cattle would be accepted; they are apparently the only breeds that have a chance of surviving the harsh Dakota winters.

July 16

We left Yankton early, and could already feel the humidity rising. Traffic was heavy as we headed to Sioux City. We were grateful to find a bike path that led us the last six miles into the city. As we leisurely biked the path along the Big Sioux River in Iowa, we stopped to take in the riverside view. Soon we were joined by a friendly, elderly cyclist dressed in well-worn, oversized jeans that were held up by bright red suspenders. It was a cycling outfit we wouldn't have chosen because the temperature was over ninety-five degrees. The gentleman told us he'd spent all his working years in the meat packing business, which used to be the largest employer in Sioux City. No longer! Gateway computers now lays claim to that distinction. Ted Waite, founder of Gateway, Inc., was born and raised in the Sioux City area, and he has not forgotten his roots. Our cycling companion told us the bike path we were on and the park we soon would be entering were some of the civic projects accomplished with the backing of Gateway. As we continued to chat, our cycling companion pointed to a peninsula in the river. "At the tip of it," he said, "the three states, South Dakota, Nebraska, and Iowa, converge. And so do the Missouri and Big Sioux Rivers." We listened to the old man reminisce about his youth, much of it spent on or near the Missouri

River. There had been so many changes in Sioux City over the course of his lifetime.

July 17

Our layover day in Sioux City, a large city on the western border of Iowa, was spent in air-conditioned environments. A Midwestern heat wave had settled in, and we took advantage of every cool spot we could find. We wandered malls, occasionally buying a small item: a magazine, some GU, a T-shirt. We went to a movie. We rested in our cool hotel room. We knew the next four days of cycling across Iowa would be ones in which heat and humidity would test our endurance.

We mailed our cold weather gear home, further reducing our load. No need to carry mittens when the temperature was soaring into the nineties. The remainder of the trip would be at lower elevations than those of the West, and we also were now into summertime temperatures.

As the trip progressed there was only one part of our anatomy that needed constant attention: our hands. No matter how many positions we found to put them in, the pressure we placed on them as we leaned over our bikes caused them to ache. We would constantly move our hands around—from low on the handlebars, to the bar directly in front of us, to the hoods covering the brakes, to the aerobars that stretched out over the front wheel. We found our hands were most comfortable when we wore gloves with extra thick padding. It became a layover day task: search for bike gloves with generous padding in the palm area. In Sioux City we found three pair—two in large, one in medium— and we purchased all of them. The medium size gloves were too big for me but I didn't care. My hands needed the extra protection.

As we drove around Sioux City in a rental car accomplishing our layover day tasks, David demonstrated he clearly wears different hats. While on his bicycle, he acts like a cyclist: He gives drivers hand signals so they know his intentions; he rides with the traffic and wears brightly colored clothes so drivers can see him. But put him behind the wheel of a car and he becomes a Boston driver, one who is known for aggressive behavior. Signal to change lanes? Not David. For most people a yellow light means it will soon turn to red and you should slow down and stop. For David it is a cue to speed up and make the light. The drivers of Sioux City had a daylong glimpse of what havoc a Boston driver can wreak in city traffic.

As soon as David drove a car into a parking lot he would start his search for an empty spot. The only requirement was that it be no more than five spaces away from the front door of the establishment. I kept reminding him he is very fit—why couldn't he park farther away and walk to the store? The Boston driver personality displayed itself. Competition! I can't tell you how many parking lots we circled so David could find a "winning" spot.

Just as David displayed opposing traits, depending on whether he was on his bicycle or behind the wheel of a car, we found automobile drivers also had split personalities, depending on whether they were driving in the country or in the city. As we cycled along back roads drivers waved to us, they gave us a thumbs up sign, or they shouted "Way to go!" from an open window. However, urban drivers treated us differently. No greetings. No thumbs up. No waving. It was obvious we impeded their progress as we cycled busy city streets. They honked their horns. They gave us minimum road space. For our part we tried to stay as far to the right as possible, although it made us uncomfortable. In city traffic we always unclipped our shoes from the pedals so we could quickly jump off if necessary. We kept our eyes focused on the road ahead in case a parked car had an occupant ready to open a door, forcing us to stop quickly.

By the time we got to Sioux City, we'd biked more than two thousand miles. With that distance under our belts, we felt we could reflect on what a cyclist experiences that an automobile driver, making the same trip, would not. First on our list would be that a driver does not have the opportunity to get close and personal with road kill lying in his path. We saw deer, raccoon, cats, and animals long past recognition of their living selves. The driver would miss the aroma permeating the air as he or she approached a piece of road kill. Safely enclosed in an air-conditioned environment, the driver would sail by.

Next would be seams in the road. Concrete roads are common, and the seams that are formed when one slab meets another cause a regular, monotonous thud as you cycle over them. The high-speed car buzzes over the seams, unaware. For a cyclist, the bump, bump, bump of crossing the seams is like water torture. You cycle along just waiting for the next bump. We knew the constant hitting of the seams was causing damage to our wheels, getting them out of true, but there was no way to avoid them. Touring bikes are not designed to take the stress from a road surface that feels as if you are riding over spaced-out railroad ties. We preferred smooth roads with a wide shoulder, allowing our bikes to roll freely and letting us take in the view without having to worry about potholes, cracks, or other impediments.

Further, on interstates the breakdown lanes are often lined with serrated paving, designed to wake up drivers who wander off the road. We can attest to the wake-up abilities of the serrated pavement. The loud humming noise created as you drive over the safety pavement in a car is annoying; on a bike it is bone-jarring.

Grasshoppers are something else a driver would not experience. The insects, perhaps seeking the warmth of the road, congregate there. As we cycled along, the bugs bounced off us and off of our bikes. In one area of South Dakota, the road was so heavily populated with grasshoppers that if they weren't lucky enough to bounce off our bikes, they were squashed under our wheels.

Lastly, with the continuing heat wave, we endured scorching sun. Using a sweat-proof SPF30 sunscreen was the only way we could stay outdoors without burning our skin—we did not have the protection of a car.

Automobile drivers may avoid the discomforts of being on a bicycle, but they miss far more. They don't get to be enveloped by the predawn air, the best of the day. We always welcomed our early starts because of those thirty minutes before sunrise; no other time of day could compare. Nor do the drivers see the variety of wildflowers, from the foxglove and sweet pea of the Oregon coast to the lupine of the higher elevations to the thistle and cornflowers of the plains. The constantly changing coloration and species of roadside flora were a joy. Missing for drivers would be the doe with two fawns we saw in South Dakota. Upon seeing us, one of the fawns, probably out of curiosity, started toward us. The doe, sensing her babies might be heading into trouble, followed her maternal instincts and performed incredible balletic moves, attempting to draw our attention and leave her babies in safety. She leaped fences and galloped across fields, accomplishing her mission and capturing our attention.

And we had fans! In Yankton, it was Joe Lynch from the twenty-third fire precinct in Cleveland. We met him and his family in a McDonald's as we tried to quench a heat-induced thirst. Joe was an avid cyclist and dreamed about taking a cross-country trip. At the very least, he wanted to ride his bike from Cleveland to the Black Hills of South Dakota, where his wife's relatives live and where he and his family travel each summer. He said his mother-in-law always discourages him, saying it is an impossible task. We quickly became Joe's heroes. He questioned us at length about our trip. When we got ready to leave, Joe insisted on taking our picture. As we posed in front of our bicycles, he snapped several pictures. He wanted proof for his mother-in-law that cyclists accomplish trips of great distance—and it wasn't necessary to be a teenager to do it.

Another fan was a driver who stopped his car ahead of us and hailed us over. He had been vacationing in South Dakota, camping at various sites, and had seen us several times. He assumed we were cycling to Iowa to join RAGBRAI (the *Des Moines Register's* Annual Great Bike

Race Across Iowa). His hometown was on the bike route that year, and he wanted to issue an invitation for us to stay with him and his family. When we told him about our cross-country trip and that we would not be part of RAGBRAI, he appeared disappointed.

In Sioux City, our fan was a young waitress. As we sat down to our ritual after-cycling beer, the woman noticed our sweat-stained biking attire. Or, perhaps, it was our sweaty aroma that drew her attention. When she learned we had biked to Sioux City from Oregon, she was so impressed she had to honor us in some way. Treating us to a beer was her way of saying, "Job well done."

Chapter 6
Corn...Corn...Corn

	Sioux City, Iowa, to	Miles	Elevation Gain (ft.)
July 18	Fort Dodge, Iowa	120	2,850
July 19	Waterloo, Iowa	108	1,410
July 20	Galena, Illinois	117	2,360
July 21	Bettendorf, Iowa	94	1,600
July 22	Bettendorf		Layover day
MILEAGE: 439 / ELEVATION GAIN: 8,220 FEET			

Total Mileage To Date: 2,811
Total Elevation Gain To Date: 99,740 feet

July 18

Route 20, an old two-lane road that traverses the United States, was our planned cycling route of the day: Sioux City to Fort Dodge, Iowa. It took riding just a few miles for us to realize that if we valued our lives, we would have to change roads. Route 20 in Iowa is paved with concrete, and we didn't think we could tolerate a day of hitting the seams. Traffic was heavy, but for a cyclist, the biggest problem was that Route 20 had no shoulder. If we went off the road, we landed in soft gravel. When David shouted, "Melissa, get off the road!" I quickly dismounted and ran into the gravel siding, pushing my bike. Within seconds a large truck displaying a "Wide Load" sign on the front grill and pulling a modular home passed us in the oncoming direction. At the same time, a large flatbed truck passed next to us. There was no room for us on the road. At our breakfast stop we questioned the café owner about alternate routes. He graciously outlined a route to Fort Dodge, explaining that Iowa has lightly traveled county roads that parallel the main roads. For this bit of information, we were grateful all the way across Iowa, as we found alternatives to our heavily trafficked planned routes.

Our ride through Iowa had few hills to climb. Heat and humidity, not terrain, were our challenges. A major heat wave continued with what we called the double nineties: The temperature was in the nineties, as was the relative humidity. As we cycled, our motion kept a breeze passing over us, but as soon as we stopped or slowed to start climbing, the heat bore down on us. At one stop the proprietor of a variety store took one look at us and invited us into her air-conditioned storage room, where she put a large fan directly on us. As we reclined into chairs, letting the cool air wash over us, she delivered cold drinks. David reached into his bag for money, but the clerk stopped him, saying, "The drinks are on the house. You two need them." Midwestern hospitality was something we'd heard about. Now we were getting to experience it. After that cool respite, it was difficult to leave our friendly host to get back onto our bikes, and face the unrelenting heat.

In contrast to the convenience store clerk, we discovered the manager of our motel in Fort Dodge needed a lesson in common courtesy. At check-in, we asked for a nonsmoking room. The receptionist told us our room would be on the second floor of a two-story building. We asked, "Why are the nonsmoking rooms on the second floor? Smoke rises."

The receptionist replied, "Yes, all our nonsmoking guests tell us that, but the manager feels otherwise."

We encountered the manager's style again when we used our bathroom. On the toilet tissue roll was a lockbox, the type you find in public rest rooms. He actually worried that guests would steal a roll of tissue from him. Later, as we finished dinner in the motel's dining room, we asked for dessert. Again, the manager interfered with our evening. The reply from the waitress was, "The manager says if you want dessert, you can get some Jell-O off the buffet table." Pleasing the customer was obviously not this motel manager's highest priority, unlike other Iowan business people we dealt with.

July 19

Residents of Iowa love cyclists. As we biked from Fort Dodge to Waterloo, homeowners working in their yards waved and called out to us. Many assumed we were in the state to join RAGBRAI, which draws thousands of cyclists from around the country. The great race is billed as a "moveable party," enjoyed by cycling groups and families. As we cycled, we heard shouts of "You're going in the wrong direction!" All Iowans knew RAGBRAI, which started that weekend, had a course from the western edge of Iowa to the eastern edge, and we were well past the starting line.

Iowa is corn! Corn is Iowa! We will never again think of Iowa without thinking of corn. From the western edge on the Missouri River to the eastern edge on the Mississippi River, Iowa is a sea of corn. When the wind blows, waves of green undulate across the landscape. Farm properties surrounded by tall shade trees appear as small islands in the sea of green. In the distance, large concrete grain elevators, tall cylinders grouped together, look like futuristic cities, rising high above the landscape. Iowans grow soybeans, raise hogs, and plant beans, but corn dominates. The cities are large and industrialized, containing processing plants for corn and livestock. They have manufacturing plants for farm equipment, and there are shipping concerns along the Mississippi and Missouri Rivers. But *corn* is Iowa!

Iowans either love their state, or they have an inferiority complex about it—we're not sure which. Whenever we stopped and chatted with locals, they frequently asked, "So, how do you like Iowa?" They were either seeking affirmation about how they felt about their state, or they needed confirmation their state was OK with outsiders.

The Iowans we met shared a common trait— friendliness. Iowans approached us at every stop. "Hi there! How you doing? Like Iowa?" Each time we were greeted this way, we thought of Ted, a strong, handsome young Iowan we met several years ago on the summit of a Colorado mountain. As a recent college graduate, he was taking time off so he could explore the country before settling down into a job. Together the three of us took in the spectacular mountaintop view. Ted exclaimed, "I love it here. Just look at those mountains. It's not like Iowa."

Thinking he was rejecting Iowa, I said, "You're just starting out in life. Why don't you move to Colorado?"

"Oh, no, I would never do that."

"Why?" I asked.

"I could never leave Iowa. The friendliest people on earth live in Iowa."

Now we understood.

Another idiosyncrasy of Iowans is the use of "you bet" or "you betcha" in conversation. Whenever we thanked a salesperson or waitress, the response was often "You betcha." One particular incident stood out as we crossed the state. As we sat on the steps of a variety store sipping cold drinks, several local farmers, dressed in overalls and taking a morning break, started talking with us.

"Where'd you bike from?" asked one.

"Oregon."

"How long you been on the road?" inquired another.

When David responded, "Almost five weeks," the farmer asked, "You retired?"

"No, but I planned my schedule over a year ago."

"Couldn't do that in farming."

Another remarked, "You two must have large, strong legs if you've biked here from Oregon."

As I stood up to dispose of my empty Gatorade bottle I said, "I think my legs are strong enough after five weeks of cycling."

Observing my thick, ample thighs as I approached the trash receptacle, one of the Iowan farmers opened his eyes wide, slowly shook his head from side to side, and exclaimed, "Wow, you betcha!"

July 20

The heat wave continued. Sitting in the shade during a rest stop was a necessity, but finding trees that offered a shady spot was difficult because all acreage was planted. Crawling under seven-foot-high corn offered cover from the blazing sun, but it did not offer a place to relax and stretch out. We did find places in Iowa that offered shade, though: bike trails. The best trail we found was on the day we biked from Waterloo to Galena, Illinois. At lunch in Dyerville (where the movie *Field of Dreams* was filmed), a walker told us about the Heritage Trail. It's a former railroad bed converted to a dirt trail that runs twenty-six miles to Dubuque. Nestled under the bluffs of tributaries to the Mississippi River, the trail offered us protection from the sun. We didn't care that the soft sandy surface made cycling more difficult. We willingly pushed harder on the pedals so we could stay in the shade. It was a matter of priorities. We forfeited speed to stay under those bluffs and towering trees. After a twenty-six mile ride in the comfort of shade, returning to a sun-drenched road in Dubuque was difficult.

During the heat wave it was important to stay hydrated. We found Gatorade a good source of fluids during the morning hours, but by the afternoon we could no longer tolerate its sweetness and switched to water. We drank gallons of water and still ended each day wanting more fluids. As we cycled, we were unaware of how much we were sweating. The air passing over us dried our sweat, but whenever we stopped we were wet in minutes. Water in, sweat out. It was nature's way of keeping our bodies functioning during the unbearable heat.

We crossed Iowa in three days, from Sioux City to Dubuque. In Dubuque we crossed the Mississippi River into Illinois to spend the night in Galena. Our arrival was late in the day, so we didn't have time

to meander about the charming town filled with restaurants, shops, and antique stores. From literature in our room, we learned Galena, home to Ulysses S. Grant, was the nation's largest producer of lead during the nineteenth century. With that source of wealth, Galena prospered. Many of the town's restored buildings are on the National Register of Historic Places.

July 21

We don't know what made us do it, but we developed, as we traveled, some rituals and superstitions. Our favorite ritual was the daily "high five." At the end of each cycling day, before sipping our first beer, we slapped each other's sky-reaching hand, accompanying it with a broad smile, twinkling eyes, and the mutually voiced, "Well done." Another ritual was David hollering, "Next!" when it was my turn to get into the bathroom before our pre-dawn starts. I dreaded that word each and every morning as I pulled myself into wakefulness.

David's alarm clock was the source of one of our superstitions. We discovered that whenever his alarm clock sounded more than five times before he turned it off, we had a hard day of cycling. It made getting the alarm turned off before it could strike its sixth tone imperative. Each morning, if we got to the alarm before it gave five rings, we smiled as we dressed for the day. If the rings numbered more than five, we were slow to hit the trail. When we awoke in Galena and realized the alarm had gone off more than five times, we didn't say a word to each other. We knew what lay ahead.

Our itinerary for the day was to start cycling along the Mississippi River on the eastern side. We'd cross over to the western side of the river at Clinton, Iowa and continue to Bettendorf, Iowa. We had a wonderful start along a hard-packed dirt road next to the Mississippi River, dawn just breaking in the early morning haze. It was a sight to behold: the most powerful river in the country moving along with us. After cycling ten miles, we came to a barricade of rocks three feet high, blocking the road. On top of the barricade stood a large sign: Road Closed. Having seen Road Closed signs before, we didn't let it deter us. We followed our usual course of action, which was to *go for it*. All other Road Closed signs we'd encountered were directed at automobiles, whereas we were able to get through, often walking our bicycles through construction sites. This time we were not so lucky. We walked our bikes around the barricade and in a hundred feet the road ended. The only thing beyond was a narrow path up a very steep hill. We analyzed our situation and came up with three choices. First, we could return the ten miles and start over. Second, we could hoist the bikes over a stream and walk along an active railroad track. Or, third, we could forge ahead, pushing our bikes up the steep, rocky, dirt path. Returning the ten miles was not seriously considered, nor was the idea of walking along a railroad bed. The dirt path contained tracks from mountain bikes, so we were hopeful a better path or road lay ahead. We started to hike the path, bikes by our sides. As much as I enjoy hiking, my bike with the B.O.B. carrier attached was not a good hiking companion. After an arduous struggle, during which we cursed at the difficulty and laughed at the absurdity, we managed to reach the top. Once there we cheered. The dirt road continued.

David's detailed map of Illinois did not show the break in the road. Nor did it show the dirt road getting softer, rapidly becoming loose gravel. Our cycling slowed. After some wrong turns we found someone who could give us directions. We rode several more miles of loose gravel and then coasted into Hanover, a town only eighteen miles from our starting point in Galena. We decided no more experimenting on routes. Traffic or not, we chose to stay on routes that took us directly to Bettendorf.

Our morning was wasted. The poor choice of routes caused the delay. Both of us were frustrated by our slow progress. I wanted someone to blame. But I knew David made his best attempt to get us to Bettendorf, and he was as upset as I. No whining!

As the day progressed, we continued to wish we had caught our alarm sooner. As we cycled the last miles into Bettendorf, the skies

opened up, and we rode in a drenching rain that hindered our visibility. We needed cover. Through the driving rain we saw a building off to the right. We turned off the busy highway and in minutes we were safely protected from the storm. We wiped our fog-covered glasses and looked around. We had pulled into the depot for large BFI trash trucks. How appropriate. Taking cover with smelly, dirty garbage trucks. We started laughing and couldn't stop. Was this day never to end?

We were lucky Bettendorf was a planned maintenance stop for our bicycles. At previous stops the bikes had required nothing more than cleaning and lubrication. The Bettendorf stop was different. For the last several days both of us had known our rear wheels were out of true, because our brakes had been rubbing. It was necessary for us to loosen our brakes, a dangerous situation, just to have our rear wheels turn freely. Hitting the seams in concrete roads, which put too much stress on the metal rims, caused the wheel problems. The bike mechanic took one look at our rear wheels and declared them unusable. He showed us where the metal had become cracked. Only good luck got the damaged wheels to last the distance across Iowa. Maybe our ride into Bettendorf wasn't so bad. After all, we made it!

As we left the bike shop, we realized we had avoided another potentially disastrous situation. What if a wheel had collapsed earlier in the day? What if our loose brakes had failed during the rainstorm? We put the "what ifs" aside, calling our daylong experience part of the adventure.

July 22

In Bettendorf, where we had chosen to spend a layover day, we stayed at Jumers Castle Lodge, a large Bavarian-style hotel. Dark-wood paneling, heavy damask draperies, and animal trophies hanging on the walls gave the hotel a distinctly Germanic flavor. We did not feel we were in Iowa! Our room, entirely decorated in dark red damask, had low lighting and a large valance over the king-size bed. It had the look of a brothel, but had all the amenities of a fine hotel—a collection of toiletries in the bathroom, a blow dryer, nightly turn-down service, and sweets left on the pillow.

Every few days we had a job to do: laundry. If it was a layover day, I attended to the task myself freeing David for other chores, but on the road we did laundry together. While we waited for our clothes to go through cycles in the washer and the dryer, I used the time to write on my computer, while David caught up with the latest editions of whatever newspapers he could find and his beloved *Sports Illustrated*. Until the trip, we never thought of Laundromats as places to do anything other than launder clothes. We discovered this isn't so. In Missoula, Montana, after consulting the Yellow Pages, we got the address of a Laundromat that was close to our bed and breakfast. When we arrived we became confused. Was it a Laundromat or an ice cream shop? Turns out it was both. We enjoyed ice cream cones as we laundered our clothes. In Bettendorf, the Laundromat shared space with a sports bar. It was too early in the morning for me to imbibe, but not for other customers. They downed beers to the cheers of excited soccer fans on the large TV, a constant hum from the adjacent washers and dryers in the background.

As we cycled into more urbanized sections of the United States, we learned a few lessons. Getting into and out of cities on a bicycle is no easy feat, especially during the rush hours of early morning and late afternoon. We tried to locate back roads, and if a bike path was available, we took it. Once in a city, we examined maps and asked people about alternative, low-traffic routes around main thoroughfares.

A layover day chore for David in the Quad City area, (Bettendorf and Davenport in Iowa, Rock Island and Moline in Illinois), was to find us a route out of town. We discovered traffic was not our only problem. There are many bridges that cross the Mississippi River, but only two of them in the Quad City area permit bicycles. The closest available biking bridge was several miles from our hotel. With a detailed map in hand, David drove a rental car along back roads and suburban streets until he got to one of the bridges that allowed bicycles. Once he crossed the Mississippi into Illinois, he bobbed and weaved his way around back roads to get to our planned route into Peru.

David celebrated his birthday in Bettendorf. We wanted to mark the occasion with a boat ride on the Mississippi. Because the humidity was so high, visibility dropped to several hundred feet, so sightseeing was not possible. But we couldn't leave Bettendorf without spending some time on or near the river. We opted for lunch at a riverside restaurant. As we ate, we watched coupled barges, stacked high with cargo and pushed by tugboats, pass through the system of locks that move vessels up and down the massive river.

In Bettendorf we had reserved a rental car so we could run errands, do laundry, and fine-tune the next leg of the trip. But when we went to pick it up, the rental agency could not find our reservation, and they told us they had only one car left in their lot. We took it. It was a bright red Camaro convertible, the perfect car for David, as he once again celebrated his twenty-ninth birthday. David's philosophy is, "You are only as old as you act." As he sped around Bettendorf in the car most desired by teenage boys, he felt years melt away. He was sixteen again!

Chapter 7

Canal Routes of the Midwest

	Bettendorf, Iowa, to	Miles	Elevation Gain (ft.)
July 23	Peru, Illinois	102	1,940
July 24	Bradley, Illinois	84	900
July 25	Logansport, Indiana	106	500
July 26	Fort Wayne, Indiana	78	940
July 27	Fort Wayne	Layover day	
MILEAGE: 370 / ELEVATION GAIN: 4,280 FEET			

Total Mileage To Date: 3,181
Total Elevation Gain To Date: 104,020 feet

July 23

The morning we left Bettendorf for Peru we were on the road earlier than usual. We wanted to give ourselves as much time as possible to navigate our complex route before the morning rush hour started. To speed our exit, David memorized the series of left and right turns to get us on the road to Peru. A bike trail was our starting point. From there I just followed. After twenty-two miles, which included cycling on a narrow sidewalk on a bridge crossing the Mississippi and so many turns I'd stopped counting, David proudly announced, "We are on the route to Peru!" I congratulated him on his navigational skills.

As we cycled east away from the Mississippi River, old canals paralleled our route. The canals are no longer in use for transportation,

and the areas surrounding the locks have been developed into parks. We took a break at one of them. An informational sign explained how mules, attached to barges with long ropes, would walk along the canal paths, pulling the barges. Many of those old canal paths are being converted into bike paths. We left the park with newfound appreciation of the importance of the Mississippi River to early travel and commerce.

In Peru we saw our first town that had been "malled." As we cycled in, we were charmed by the downtown, but as we rode along the main street we realized many of the stores were vacant. Interstate 80, one of the major cross-country routes, passes several miles north of town. Many of Peru's businesses have moved to the mall at the interstate exit to take advantage of the increase in traffic. Peru was one of many towns we traveled through that had changed dramatically because of the development of a mall. As we cycled into the centers of these towns, a quick glance around confirmed for us whether or not a mall existed somewhere nearby.

A sign, advertising a restaurant called the Red Door Inn caught our eye as we cycled into Peru. The sign said the restaurant offered fine dining with views overlooking the Illinois River. Although we stayed in a motel next to the interstate (because we had no downtown choices), we planned to take a cab and return to the inn for dinner. As we stood on a sidewalk in Peru, deciding how to spend the remainder of the afternoon, a middle-aged gentleman approached us. We chatted for a minute, and then asked him about the Red Door Inn. He took one look at us, sweaty and in biking attire, and said, "Oh, no, you don't want to go there. It's expensive and you have to dress up. There's a pizza parlor a block away that's not too expensive, and they make their own pizza from scratch!" It was not the first time someone had judged us by our attire. People assumed that because we were on bicycles we needed to find budget food. I suppose they thought that if we could afford expensive food, we could afford a car to travel in.

That evening at the Red Door Inn, we enjoyed talking with our young waiter, who was an accomplished tableside cook. Thinking it unusual that someone eighteen years old was good at preparing steak Diane, Caesar salad and crepes Suzette, we asked him about his cooking skills. We learned his parents were friends of the restaurant owners, who had offered him a job before he went off to college in the fall. The young man enjoyed good food, so he thought it natural that he should learn how to prepare it. He took some cooking lessons and here he was.

We continued to talk with the young man as he prepared our anchovy-rich Caesar salad. He told us tableside cooking was a better job than the one he'd had the previous summer: cutting the tassels off corn. We had never heard of that job and thought the young man was jesting with us. Although our tableside chef could not explain what lopping off the corn tassel achieved, he thought it had something to do with avoiding reproduction. After that lesson in corn cultivation, we noticed many acres of corn missing their tassels.

We took a memory of this charming young man with us for the remainder of the trip: While flambéing our crepes Suzette, our young chef's flair became overzealous and some of the sweet, orange sauce spilled on David's only pair of dress pants. Although we tried to remove the spot with spit, and then with water, it remained lodged on his right pant leg. The stain provided a memory of the Red Door Inn and our friendly waiter until the pants reached the dry cleaners at home.

July 2

In Braidswood, Illinois, we crossed historic Route 66, the renowned
highway from Chicago to Los Angeles that Nat King Cole made famous
in the song "Get your Kicks on Route 66" and was the inspiration for
the '60s TV series *Route 66*. It was lunchtime, so we stopped at the Polka
Dot Drive-In. We felt we had stepped back in time. It was the '50s. We
were teenagers again. Food could be ordered by shouting into speakers
next to parked cars, or patrons could order while sitting inside at tables,
listening to rock'n'roll blaring from a jukebox. Posters of Elvis and Betty
Boop covered the walls. A large sign advertised that the Polka Dot was
sponsoring a "Cruisin' night" the next week in which cars from the
fifties would be judged in various categories—convertibles, two-door
sedans, and four-door sedans.

While David ordered our lunch, I looked around at the Polka
Dot's customers. Seated in the next booth was an elderly couple,
accompanied by, I assumed, several grandchildren. What made the
couple noteworthy was their appearance. The woman's white hair was
pulled back into a tight bun, a severe part down the center of her head.
Her dress was a housecoat— a small floral print cotton garment— that
buttoned the entire way down the front. And she had on sensible shoes—
laced-up black ones, with just a minimum of heel. Her husband was
dressed in well-worn, oversized woolen pants that were kept up with
the widest pair of red suspenders I'd ever seen. Underneath the
suspenders he wore the top from a long-john set. And on his feet, tie-
up boots. They were dressed like a farm couple from an earlier time.
It was quite a contrast—their garments against the stylish jeans, messaged
T-shirts and up-to-date athletic shoes of their grandchildren.

After a lunch of burgers and shakes (what else would a teen of the
fifties have?), we retired to our respective restrooms. David took his time.
When he finally returned, I questioned him. "What took you so long?"

A sly smile, accompanied by raised eyebrows, was his answer.

I questioned him again. "Seriously, are you sick? Is that why you
took so long?"

His smile got larger and he raised his eyebrows again, Groucho Marx style. Obviously something good had happened. Through his mischievous smile he said, "I just spent time with Marilyn Monroe. The men's room is lined with photos. I had to check 'em out."

This might be the only restroom in the nation where the wait for the men's room is as long as it is for the women's room.

On the ride into Bradley, Illinois, we were disappointed, but it had nothing to do with the town. Our disappointment had occurred during the planning of the trip. As David researched various inn guides he found a listing for Yesteryear, an inn situated in Kankakee, the town next to Bradley. The eighteen-room inn, designed by the architect Frank Lloyd Wright in the Prairie School Style, was constructed in 1900. David rerouted the trip so we would pass through Kankakee and enjoy a night's stay in a Frank Lloyd Wright creation. But when I called the inn to make a reservation, I discovered it had closed several years earlier. The current residents directed me to the motel in Bradley where we ended up staying.

In Bradley, we met another fan. The young girl who checked us in to the motel inquired about our trip and was astounded to learn we had biked to Bradley from Oregon. She kept looking at us, asking, "How far did you say you biked?" When we told her more than three thousand miles, she exclaimed, "You two are amazing! You belong in the *Guinness Book of World Records*." When we explained to her that many people cycle across the United States, she almost told us why she was impressed by our accomplishment. "But both of you are…" and she stopped. Her face said it all: *old*!

July 25

In selecting biking apparel for the trip, we purchased only clothes that were brightly colored. Wearing them would provide drivers an opportunity to see us from a distance. We also had flashing red lights mounted below our bike seats, which we turned on during periods of low visibility. On the morning we left Bradley for Logansport, Indiana, we were glad we'd chosen to wear our screaming yellow jerseys. The humidity was high, causing a thick fog to form against the cooler ground. We could have sliced it with a knife. With our red lights flashing, we cycled close together. We were fortunate it was early and traffic was light—the fog was so thick we heard cars before we saw them. As soon as the sun rose, the heavy ground fog burned off and we continued our journey, happy that good visibility had returned.

Days passed quickly. We biked. We slept. We ate. Breakfast was our favorite meal. We usually had miles completed before we took a breakfast break. By the time we stopped, food consumption was mandatory. Pancakes, French toast, eggs, omelets, sausage, bacon, toast—everything tasted wonderful.

With our exercised-induced hunger we ate food that hadn't crossed our lips in years. The best of these were doughnuts. At a roadside café the day we cycled into Logansport, we ordered an "energy breakfast"— eggs, pancakes or French toast and a breakfast meat. But when we discovered the café specialized in homemade doughnuts, their freshly fried aroma filling the restaurant, we succumbed. Each of us quickly devoured a cinnamon crusted doughnut. What a taste treat! Homemade cinnamon rolls, their glaze warmed to a gooey, sticky consistency, were another Midwestern treat. Whenever we found them on a menu, we added their extra calories to our meal. We never stepped on a scale during the trip, but we knew we were not losing weight. We hoped we were adding muscle. As the trip continued, we feared our eating binge would be difficult to stop. Daily we craved those calories!

As we cycled across Illinois and Indiana, we found the landscape continued to be dominated by farms, but they differed from the ones in Iowa. No longer were corn and soybeans the only crops grown. We could smell air laced with sweet basil, young scallions, ripening melons, and fragrant flowers. Towns and cities appeared with more regularity. Traffic on the roads was heavier. The most noticeable change for us was the return of trees. Not all land was farmed, as it was in Iowa; on some back roads we rode beneath a canopy of trees, and it was wonderful to escape the sun's constant rays.

After being on the road for several weeks, we found ourselves in need of a haircut. But finding someone to give us a haircut was a challenge. We likened it to playing roulette: Winning meant getting a good hair stylist. Both of us have difficult hair. Mine is ample but fine. It took my hair stylist at home months to learn where all the cowlicks are. My bangs are a special problem: they want to swing in one direction and refuse to lie straight; layering is the only solution. When I stepped out of one hair salon in Indiana I was close to tears. Despite my directions to the young stylist, my bangs were too short. They stood straight out, reminding me of the way I used to cut my daughters' bangs. I'd stick Scotch tape across their foreheads to form a straight line and then, with one quick nip of the scissors, whack off the hair. The results were usually so disastrous my daughters were ecstatic when I gave up and sent them off to a beauty salon. I now could relate to their feelings.

David had submitted his head of hair to a barber back in Iowa. When he stepped out of the shop looking like a fresh Marine's recruit, we took the expression "a good haircut is only a week away from a bad haircut" to heart. Except in his case we thought two weeks would be needed. We both were thankful we had bike helmets to hide our poorly cut hair.

David and I underwent significant personality changes during our odyssey. Prior to this trip, David would *never* ask anyone for directions. It didn't matter that we would be late for an appointment; it made no difference when I offered to do the asking, saving face for him. He still refused to ask for directions. He preferred to put his faith in his map-reading and navigation skills. His rallying cry was always, "Just let me look at the map!" However, after using some of his highly detailed maps, which didn't differentiate between paved and unpaved surfaces, David learned to ask people about the road conditions ahead. That led to questions about our destination for the day. The respondent often gave David a better route for cyclists, one that had better views, avoided construction areas, or had a better road surface. The two of them, inquirer and respondent, stood talking, the local displaying his knowledge of the area and David relating his travel experiences.

Another change for David was his willingness to strike up conversations. I have always been the one to open the door to conversation. I would question the couple sitting next to us in a restaurant or make a remark to a youngster who was cycling beside us. Perhaps it was David's need to speak to someone other than me that encouraged his openness with people. At a breakfast stop in Indiana, David spent the entire time conversing with a World War II veteran. Battle of the Bulge, D-Day, excursions through Italy—all made their way into the conversation. I was left alone to eat my pancakes.

The big change I made was I no longer was a whiner. I didn't complain about the heat. I didn't gripe about the length of a cycling day. I took on hills with a smile. I displayed constant enthusiasm.

I found that if I thought of other things, not concentrating on cycling, the day passed quickly, heat and all. I never was bored. Thoughts played through my mind as I mentally wrote in my journal. Each day I had to think about what I wanted to put on our Web page. When I spoke with our daughter Stephanie, she said she could always recognize the Web notes I spent time laboring over. She laughed over characters I painted. She enjoyed the scenes I created. She felt the enthusiasm David and I had as we made our way across the country.

Although I spent many cycling hours creating and refining what to offer my Internet audience, I also spent time thinking about our daughters and their families. I was thankful each was married and settled into a good life. Although our daughters have gone in different directions, professionally and geographically, whenever we come together as a family we still share laughter. Fortunately, our three sons-in-law have seamlessly entered our active family.

As I pedaled along, I loved reliving the hasty visit we had with our grandchildren at the start of the trip. I recalled granddaughter Serena's begging, "Gammy, play patty-cake, patty-cake," and seeing her laughing face as we finished reciting the verse together. I remembered grandson Trés hollering, "Find me! Find me!" as he tucked himself behind a shrub and I was left scrambling among the evergreens looking for him.

I thought of friends and family, especially when I wanted to share a special part of the trip. I wanted friends to see the farm couple at the Polka Dot Drive-in who could have walked out of Grant Wood's painting, *American Gothic*. I wanted to share the humidity-filled dawn as we cycled along the Mississippi River near Galena, Illinois. The scene could have been lifted from a Joseph Turner painting of the Thames River as it weaved its way into London. I wanted friends to experience the interesting people we met: David's talkative World War II veteran, the group of farmers outside the convenience store in Iowa, the daredevil crop duster from Cody, Wyoming who wanted to give us a lift over the Big Horn Mountains. I wanted family and friends to know how often I thought of them as we cycled this great country.

Frequently when I looked ahead and saw David, I thought how fortunate we were to be able to make this trip. Our responsibilities as parents were over. We were now in the joyful phase of child rearing—we were grandparents. Our health was good. And we were still capable of putting in long days of cycling. David calls this phase of life our golden years.

A memory game was another way to occupy my mind. We'd traveled far enough that mentally reconstructing the trip, day by day, was a challenge. As I thought of each day I tried to recollect our destination, our accommodations, and where we'd had dinner. When I was unable to reconstruct each breakfast and luncheon spot, David offered his help. After accomplishing this, I performed my super-challenge memory game: I reconstructed the trip backward! That must have been my brain cells craving exercise, something they hadn't had in six weeks.

July 26

Back in the eighties, when the Boston Celtics were regularly in contention for the NBA championship, Celtics star Larry Bird said he enjoyed playing in the non-air-conditioned Boston Garden in June. He loved it as the temperature in the Garden climbed to 104 degrees. He said it reminded him of home—Indiana. Perhaps if we had been raised in Indiana's brutally hot summer climate, we would have biked better. As we slowly cycled into Fort Wayne's airport to pick up our rental car, the official heat index was 110 degrees. It was the hottest day either of us had ever experienced.

Advertising does pay! Several days in advance of each layover day, we made reservations for a rental car. Before the trip I used to hear radio advertisements by Enterprise car rental whose biggest advantage over the competition was that they would deliver the rental car to your destination and pick it up as well. It was the perfect arrangement for us. Up to this point in the trip, we'd rented most of our cars from Enterprise. This time we hadn't planned properly. Enterprise doesn't perform its delivery service after noon on Saturdays, and we had arrived in Fort Wayne at two o'clock in the afternoon. Our only chance of renting a car was from an agency at the Fort Wayne airport. That required us to rent a boat of a car—a Lincoln Continental— so we could get both our bikes in the trunk and drive to our motel.

While David went into the terminal to make arrangements for the car, I slumped down on the pavement outside, leaned my head back against the brick wall and closed my eyes. A police officer patrolling the drop off area stopped and inquired, "Are you all right?"

Startled, I opened my eyes, answering, "Yeah, I guess so. It's just so hot. I don't know how you stand being outside."

"I'm not biking. And I can slip inside the air-conditioned terminal anytime I want."

"I wish we were back in the mountains of the West. There it was so cool we had to wear leggings and a jacket. Even mittens."

"I'm getting out of this heat for two weeks, starting tomorrow. My wife and I are taking our Gold Wing motorcycle and heading west. We're not stopping until we find cooler weather," he said.

I envied him. I wasn't sure I could take another day of the penetrating heat.

July 27

Fort Wayne was not a scheduled bike maintenance stop, but David's bike needed some work. Unfortunately, a summer Sunday in Fort Wayne was not a good time to find open bike shops. We tried the bike shop near our motel, but a sign on the door said that Sundays were reserved for riding. After calling the remaining bike shops in the Yellow Pages, we found one whose phone message said they would be opening at one o'clock. We sat in their parking lot praying the phone message was for that day. We silently cheered as we saw the shop lights go on and the bike mechanic waved us inside.

We learned from our experience in Fort Wayne that we shouldn't have planned layover days for weekends. We never thought about the chores we needed to accomplish on our days off. Our thought when we planned the trip was to sightsee on layover days. As we soon learned, layover days were not just for sightseeing, but for catching up as well. David would call his office, so weekends were not a good time to connect with colleagues. For us, each day of the trip was a vacation day so why schedule layover days on the weekend?

The receptionist at our motel recommended Café Jonnell for dinner, saying it was one of the finest restaurants in Fort Wayne. As we drove to the restaurant, we thought the neighborhood was not a likely candidate for a top-rated restaurant. We were wrong. The neighborhood surrounding Café Jonnell was a bit run-down, but the food was authentic French gourmet. We learned Café Jonnell was an institution in Fort

Wayne dining. We savored every bite of our dinners, from smoked salmon appetizers to chocolate and fresh raspberry desserts. We agreed with the many Holiday Fine Dining awards that covered the walls.

Another treat of Café Jonnell was we got to order a bottle of wine by its variety. The wine list contained Chardonnays, Merlots, Cabernet Sauvignons, and Burgundies. In many dining places we'd been to, wine was not the preferred drink to accompany food, and what wines they had we selected by color: red, white, or pink. In one restaurant, after sipping a startling cold glass of red wine, I called the waitress over to our table. I inquired, "Could I possibly get a glass of red wine that is not so chilled?"

When the waitress returned, she explained, "The bartender can't serve wine at room temperature. Once the cardboard carton of wine is open, it has to stay refrigerated."

The extreme heat did not abate during our layover day. We spent most of our time exploring Fort Wayne from the seats of our air-conditioned car. We prayed for a storm to clear out the heat and humidity before we continued our journey into Ohio. As we stepped out from an early evening movie, dark clouds approached and flashes of lightning illuminated the sky. We cheered! The heat wave had finally broken. We knew the next day was going to be a good one!

Chapter 8
Buckeye State

Fort Wayne, Indiana, to		Miles	Elevation Gain (ft.)
July 28	Defiance, Ohio	57	90
July 29	Bowling Green, Ohio	53	260
July 30	Oberlin, Ohio	96	790
July 31	Painesville, Ohio	90	3,280
Aug 1	Painesville	Layover day	

MILEAGE: 296 / ELEVATION GAIN: 4,420 FEET

Total Mileage To Date: 3,477
Total Elevation Gain To Date: 108,440 feet

July 28

Fort Wayne was our last struggle with urbanization. While I did my
layover day chore, the laundry, David drove our rented Lincoln
Continental around back roads, plotting our course for leaving heavily
trafficked Fort Wayne. We successfully negotiated his route as the sun
was rising on a clear, cool day—the first we'd had since leaving the Big
Horn Mountains of Wyoming.

It was a short, flat ride into Defiance, Ohio. As we cycled along
the main road entering Defiance, we got our first visible sign we were
heading home: there, surrounded by a parking lot filled with cars, was
a Friendly's. The restaurant chain has shops all around the Northeast

and, as we discovered, as far west as Defiance, Ohio. We were surprised at how excited we got seeing evidence that we were closing in on the finish. Our spirits soared. We rushed inside and placed an order. With vivid memories of our teenage dating years, we ordered flavored Fribbles, the extra thick shakes that are a Friendly's trademark. David got a strawberry one; I chose coffee. The dilemma of trying to consume a Fribble was still the same—sip it through a straw or eat it with a spoon? The waitress delivered both, so we could make our own decision.

Our early arrival gave us the afternoon to explore Defiance. Our first stop was the public library, where we hoped to find a computer that was connected to the Internet. When we spoke to people back home, they told us how much they enjoyed reading our Web page, and we hadn't even seen it. Friends told us how Sean Nolan had created an interesting Norton Cross-Country Web site: Upon logging on, a large calendar greeted the user. Days on which I had posted information were highlighted, and if a user double-clicked on the date, my e-mail notes were displayed. Sean created links to Web sites of cities we passed through. A visitor to our site could discover places worth visiting in Sioux City, Iowa, or learn the current temperature in Fort Wayne, Indiana.

All the computers at the Defiance library were busy. I went over to the resource librarian and described our situation, and she was willing to help us. On her desk sat a computer for her exclusive use. She said if I would tell her what to do, we could display our Web site on the screen. Step by step I walked her through the process. Double-click on that icon. Go to the menu and select that command. Type in these words. It was only seconds before a photo of me pulling the B.O.B. carrier was digitally created on her computer's monitor. The librarian, with an amazed look on her face, exclaimed, "Why that's you! How did you do that?" I told her how I sent information via e-mail and Sean posted it. Together, we and the librarian explored our Web site. The librarian did not want us to leave. She was learning, through our Web site, how to navigate the Net.

As we cycled around Defiance, we enjoyed the freedom of biking without packs. Our legs loved it. We loved it. I kept thinking it must be the same feeling an adult male moose or elk gets as he drops his heavy winter rack. At once movement is easier. Nothing constrains you. But just as moose and elk get a new rack, we again became beasts of burden, bearing our heavy loads.

In the park outside the library, where the Maumee and Auglaize Rivers converge, we learned Defiance was named for Fort Defiance. "I defy the English, the Indians and all the devils in hell to take it," said the fort's commander, General Anthony Wayne in 1794. Forces from the fort expelled all Native Americans from the Northwest Territories, which in colonial times included Ohio.

A loudspeaker bellowing across the park, announcing the starting lineup for the Mudhens, awakened us from our riverside naps. We excitedly headed toward the park's baseball field. An afternoon of watching the Triple-A Toledo Mudhens would be a treat. As we approached the field, we saw few fans. Players were no taller than five feet. The Mudhens were a Little League team. We joined the players' parents and relatives in the stands.

David, a former Little Leaguer, became engrossed in the error-ridden play of the youngsters. I was intrigued by the actions of the young players. As I continued to watch, I found I could predict a player's response as the ball came his way. With each skittering of the ball between legs or high throw over outstretched hands, the young player who had committed the error would look at his coach. Then he would cross clenched fists across his chest, stamp his foot on the ground and holler something sounding like, "Aw, shucks!" Not one player followed the ball with the intention of rescuing the situation. We left after the third inning, and as we walked away, we heard a woman in the stands scream in an ear-piercing tone. "Charlie, go after that ball! Yes, Charlie, this is your mama talking to you!"

July 29

As we continued across Ohio, cycling to the university town of Bowling Green, we rode through towns resembling those of our native New England. Centrally located town greens, stately courthouses, large town halls, and spired churches were common. Roads started to meander, no longer defined by a grid. Barns were painted red. Towns were closer together. The New Englanders who settled Ohio, seeking better farmland, had brought their traditions with them.

Most of the towns we cycled through in Ohio had not succumbed to a mall. The downtown areas were lively, serving the needs of the populace. As we cycled into Napolean, we were struck by the town's charm. It had extensive parks, a lengthy bike route into town, and tidy, well-kept homes. And it had an additional attribute: It smelled divine! As we rode the bike path into town, the aroma of cooking vegetables aroused our appetites. We could smell broccoli, spinach, onions, and mushrooms, all mingled together to create the kitchen aromas of a serious chef. And the wonderful aromas continued as we rode out of town. Before long we observed a large complex of buildings with steam spouting from a dozen or so stacks. The air couldn't have smelled better. As we closed in on the building complex, we read the large sign at the gate. Napoleon, Ohio, is home of Campbell's Soup Company.

As we continued to Bowling Green, we passed through Grand Rapids, an attractive town on the Maumee River. We immediately recognized it as a tourist town, because it had five craft stores, two ice cream parlors, and three restaurants, all close together, but no hardware store or grocery market. When we asked a visitor what was Grand Rapids' attraction, she responded, "It's a restored canal town." We took part of the afternoon to explore the old canal that carried cargo and passengers from Toledo to Cincinnati. As part of the tourist attraction, a canal boat, using a team of mules, was available for a short ride along the restored canal. Travel along canals was short-lived, lasting about twenty years during the early nineteenth century, before rail travel became available. At the leisurely pace of four miles an hour, canal travel was unable to compete with the railroads.

In Grand Rapids, I attracted another fan. As I was leaving the old canal site, I met two couples who were traveling around Ohio by car. I spoke with them about our trip, and one of the gentlemen asked me if I was cycling alone. As I replied "No," David, who was still off exploring the canal site, came into view.

The gentleman, observing David, said in jest, "Oh, you're a father-daughter team." I couldn't resist: For the remainder of the day, I called David *"Dad"*. That was short-lived, as I wanted a companion for the remainder of the trip.

While sitting on a bench outside a Grand Rapids ice cream shop, we met our most memorable fan. He was a toothless, smiling little man, a fellow soldier of the road, who rode a heavy one-speed roadster bicycle. David and I silently looked at each other and mouthed, "Rocket Man". That is the affectionate name we've applied over the years to any lone cyclist whose bike is his only means of transportation. Our Grand Rapids Rocket Man joined us on the bench, and we compared cycling equipment and related biking stories.

His heavy roadster had a mirror, six inches by twelve inches, attached by heavy steel piping to the left side of his handlebars. He proudly told us, "It's the rear view mirror from a truck. Found it in the junkyard."

His bike's front and rear wheel covers had large mud flaps, adorned with the gun-blazing cartoon character Yosemite Sam, and the message "Back Off." Again, "Found 'em at the dump."

Wired to his handlebar were dozens of the Veteran's of Foreign Wars red paper poppies. I asked. "Are you a veteran?"

"No, just like to decorate my bike. Want one?"

David and I each accepted a red paper poppy.

On the rear of his bike our Rocket Man carried two large wire baskets filled with empty cans and bottles. He provided a service—

keeping the roads clean for cyclists. Our cycling friend's name should have been on one of those highway markers outside Grand Rapids, claiming the next two miles are kept clean by "Rocket Man".

After hearing about our lengthy trip, our cycling companion said he wanted to join us on the road. When we told him our destination for the day, Bowling Green, was thirty miles away, he declined, saying, "I've never biked that far. But some day I'm going to."

July 30

As we moved across Ohio into the pretty town of Oberlin, another change in scenery struck us. With greater frequency we saw "those expensive foreign cars." That is how a westerner we met described the BMWs, Mercedes, Volvos, and Porsches we saw cruising along the highways. Throughout the West and Midwest, American-made vehicles are prevalent. *"Buy American"* is a popular bumper sticker. Affluence is not displayed by driving an expensive foreign car. Perhaps it is demonstrated by acreage, size of cattle herds, or miles of elaborate fencing, but it is not by driving an expensive foreign car.

On a road outside Oberlin, we stopped to chat with a college student who had been cycling out of town. As we discussed our trip, he brazenly asked, "How old are you?"

Startled, I responded, "He's fifty-six. I won't be fifty-six for a few more weeks."

"You guys are older than my parents. I can't picture them doing a cycling trip."

"It really isn't difficult once you get yourself in shape," David told him. "If you can bike twenty miles, you can bike a hundred. Once in shape, it's your head that takes over. So much of long-distance cycling is convincing your body it can go the distance."

"I can't wait to tell my parents about you. I've been trying to get them off their butts and do some exercising," responded the student.

We arrived in Oberlin early enough to have time for a walking tour of the town and the campus of Oberlin College. We had a mission to accomplish: Some friends of ours spent their first years of marriage in Oberlin, where she was a student and he worked for NASA. They had not been back to Oberlin since those early years, and they wanted to know if their apartment house was still there—and if so, what was its condition? Camera in hand, we sought out the early twentieth-century home that was divided into student apartments. Good news! The building survives. We took pictures as proof that 82 East College Street still serves the student population of Oberlin College.

July 31

Flat terrain continued across Ohio until we reached the outskirts of Cleveland. Our destination was Painesville, a city east of Cleveland on Lake Erie. Cleveland is fortunate to have a series of parks that ring the metropolitan area to the south. The parks, all linked, are appropriately called Cleveland's Emerald Necklace. For the first time since leaving the Oregon Coast, we cycled through a heavily forested hilly landscape. At lunch, the clerk at the deli counter told us Cleveland, whose trees were felled to accommodate a growing population, was once known as "The Forest City." The parks give evidence as to how treed the landscape once was. For much of the day, we biked from one park to the next, not feeling we were close to a large city. We had not climbed any major hills since leaving Wyoming. As we cycled park roads, with names such as Overlook Drive and Gorge Highway, we prepared ourselves for the remainder of the trip. We knew hills were back, and they wouldn't cease until we reached the Atlantic Ocean.

We left Cleveland's park system to cycle along Chagrin River Road, where it was difficult to keep our eyes on the road. Stately gated mansions lined our route, and we had fun critiquing the various styles of architecture and landscapes the mansions presented. We slowed down and took our time, looking at each home.

It was late in the afternoon when I succumbed: I finally met a hill I couldn't cycle; the pitch of the steep, short hill was too much for me. Luckily, I remembered my friend Lee's adage, "I've never met a hill I couldn't walk." So I dismounted and walked, pushing the bike and the B.O.B. carrier. As I struggled up the steep incline, I kept hoping the remainder of the trip offered no more challenges like the hills surrounding Cleveland.

Later we had another problem. It was bound to happen when nine weeks of hotel and inn reservations are made six months in advance. After ninety arduous miles, we reached Painesville and stepped into the lovely, quaint Ryder's 1812 Inn to claim our room for the next two days. After a search of the registry, the desk clerk told us she didn't have our reservation. Perhaps it was the heat of the day or the length of the day or that I was just plain angry, but I lit into the staff. "What do you mean you can't honor this reservation? I made it six months ago!"

Whenever I made a room reservation, I got a confirmation number or the name of a person who could vouch for the reservation. Wisely, I carried this list with me. I gave the business manager's name, and there was no denying she'd accepted the reservation. As the manager's secretary told us, she'd probably written it on a piece of paper, to be recorded later. And later never happened.

Because there was a fishing derby on Lake Erie, all the rooms at Ryder's Inn were booked. Realizing the business manager had made a mistake, the staff proposed to solve our dilemma. As David contacted Enterprise car rental, I sat in the bar fuming. The staff offered me shrimp cocktail and cold beer. I angrily refused both. Shortly, another staff person returned to inform me she'd booked us into a discount motel on the interstate. I blew my stack! I informed the growing crowd that Painesville was a layover day for us, and we did not want to spend it in a discount motel. We did our research and sought out Ryder's, with its character and historical significance. (We already knew Ryder's, with a maze of tunnels beneath it, was a safe house on the Underground

Railroad, for slaves escaping from the South.) My outcry was gaining me sympathy from the bar's patrons, but the staff had had enough of me. They assigned a waitress to sit with me. She empathized with our situation—on bicycles, tired, hungry, and no room at the inn. Meanwhile, phone calls were being made. Finally, the Ryder's staff offered a solution I accepted. They'd booked us into Quail Hollow, a golf resort not far away, with the first night compliments of Ryder's.

Getting ready for dinner at Quail Hollow, David and I discussed my behavior in the bar of Ryder's Inn. David had been embarrassed by my outburst. It was totally out of character for me. Direct aggressive confrontation is not how I deal with problems. I use the quiet, rational approach. To this day, I don't know what came over me. Was I so exhausted I forgot myself? Did the idea of getting back on my bicycle after that long day overcome me?

The restaurant at Quail Hollow offered us some of the best food we'd had on the trip. My earlier outburst was quickly forgotten as we sipped a wonderful Chardonnay and ate fresh salmon covered with a mustard-dill sauce. We put aside our craving for beef for this taste treat. The evening was so enjoyable, we canceled our plans to dine the next night in Cleveland and returned to the Quail Hollow restaurant.

August 1

As it turned out, we could not have found a better layover stop than Quail Hollow. It had our two requisites: air-conditioning and good food. We longed to try the links, but we knew once we got home we could play golf anytime. Days off were for seeing the sights!

Once we completed our layover day chores, we drove to Cleveland to visit the Rock and Roll Museum. Before entering the museum, we stood outside in its large plaza and marveled at the beautiful location. The Rock and Roll Museum and the Cleveland Art Museum share a Lake Erie shoreline site. The glass-dominated architecture of the buildings is stunning. The Cleveland Art Museum looks like a large,

stationary ship, with decks wrapping around each level. A large, triangular sloping-glass roof dominates the entrance hall of the Rock and Roll Museum. As we entered the sun-filled museum dedicated to our generation's music, we starting snapping our fingers and swaying our hips to the beat of familiar songs flowing from a bank of speakers.

We discovered that more than an afternoon is needed to enjoy all the museum's displays. David and I separated, each looking for our favorite rock and roll star. Buddy Holly, who died tragically in a plane crash, is David's favorite. For me, it is the woman who has survived hardship and grown older, yet still sings, struts, and dances like a young woman: Tina Turner. She is my heroine!

The exhibits in the museum make extensive use of technology. One display that particularly intrigued me lets visitors hear and see the various musicians who influenced a later rock star's musical style. From this multimedia exhibit, I learned Roy Orbison was Bruce Springsteen's major influence. As your finger selects musicians pictured on a monitor, links take you to new screens where music of that musician is played. Then you can compare and contrast the musical styles of rock and roll stars from today and yesterday.

It was a large crowd that snaked its way through the five floors of exhibits, and it was a happy crowd. At each display we heard, "Yeah, yeah, yeah. I remember that!" Couples leaned into each other, bumping and grinding to the beat. Everyone was "feelin' good."

It was the first time we visited Cleveland, and both of us were impressed. From Painesville, getting into the city was quick and easy. The downtown area has many high-rise buildings, giving the city a distinctive skyline. The extensive park system, our biking route around Cleveland, is a natural jewel. And the museums along Lake Erie add architectural beauty and cultural interest to the city. Although our experience in Cleveland was limited, we liked what we saw.

Chapter 9

Land of Many Lakes

Painesville, Ohio, to		Miles	Elevation Gain (ft.)
Aug 2	Cambridge Springs, PA	81	2,450
Aug 3	Jamestown, New York	69	4,110
Aug 4	Olean, New York	76	1,820
Aug 5	Corning, New York	90	2,850
Aug 6	Geneva, New York	65	2,030
Aug 7	Pulaski, New York	99	3,150
Aug 8	Old Forge, New York	84	4,060
Aug 9	Saranac Lake, New York	92	3,930
Aug 10	Saranac Lake		Layover Day

MILEAGE: 656 / ELEVATION GAIN: 24,400 FEET

Total Mileage To Date: 4,133
Total Elevation Gain To Date: 132,840 feet

August 2

Hills were back! Because they were, David lowered the daily mileage for our travel in Pennsylvania and New York. We didn't mind the return of hills. For each significant gain in elevation, we got a restful downhill, and we hadn't coasted for weeks. Throughout the flat Midwest, we had to stay on the pedals. No resting! It was a treat to relax and look out over the landscape as we rolled down a long hill.

We'd stopped using our self-planned route back in Indiana, returning to Adventure Cycling's northern tier maps. On this popular route, people are used to seeing cyclists on the road. As we negotiated our way to Cambridge Springs, Pennsylvania, a gentleman who was gardening in his yard motioned for us to stop. He said he stops all passing cyclists to warn them about the steep climbs ahead on the Adventure Cycling route. His recommendation was to take the main highway, avoiding the hills. Most cyclists take his advice. We were not in the mood to ride with fast moving traffic, so we opted to climb the hills. After cycling the Big Horn Mountains in Wyoming, with a constant 10 percent grade, we jokingly called all other hills "wee-wees." These hills were nothing to worry about. Except for the "walking hill" outside of Cleveland, I had climbed all hills. David's record was 100 percent.

Shortly after we cycled into northwest Pennsylvania, we stopped to read a roadside historical marker. We were standing in the spot where oil was first found, leeching its way to the earth's surface. The prospector, who was searching for salt, knew of no use for oil and continued his search for salt. A major missed opportunity.

South of our route, in Titusville, Pennsylvania, Edwin Drake discovered oil in 1859. At that time, oil that had seeped to the surface

was being used in lamps and as a lubricant for machinery, but there was no readily available supply. Drake discovered a way to pump the oil from the ground and the oil boom was on. Evidence of the early drilling still exists. Fields, which are hayed or planted with corn, have rusting oil-pump jacks strewn throughout, and old storage tanks line the road.

The receptionist at the Riverside Inn gave us a suspicious look as we checked in. She repeated several times the dress policy for the hotel's dining room: men *must* wear pants, not shorts or jeans. A jacket was not necessary. A large sign displayed outside the dining room, stating the hotel's dress policy, was pointed out to us more than once. Did we look that bad? Did she think we would present ourselves for dinner in our biking attire? We assured her we "clean up good," and we would not be a source of embarrassment to the inn.

Whenever we got a worried look from hotel personnel, we recalled an experience we had on a weekend bike trip. As we checked into a beautiful Vermont inn, we were cordially greeted by the innkeepers. They offered us lemonade, cookies, and conversation. After finishing our snack, we went to our room to get ready for dinner.

On our arrival we had not been a pretty sight. After showers our hair was no longer matted to our heads, soaked with sweat. The chain grease that usually lines our right calves was scrubbed away. The road dirt and the salty crust of dried sweat were washed off. David's day old stubble of beard was shaved clean.

Later that evening, as we sat on the front porch, one of the innkeepers greeted us and inquired if we had checked in yet. By her question it was obvious she didn't recognize us! Her face flushed when I told her we were the cyclists she'd spoken with an hour earlier. "But you look so different!" she exclaimed. Because of our Vermont inn experience, we tell hotel staffers apprehensive about our dirty, smelly appearance that we "clean up good."

The discovery of mineral water in Cambridge Springs in the late nineteenth century was responsible for the creation of the resort town. The medicinal properties of the mineral water were praised, and patrons arrived so they could "take the waters." The Riverside Inn is the lone survivor of that era, in continuous operation since 1884. The hotel has reinvented itself as a weekend getaway, offering an old-world setting for weddings and conferences. Another large draw for the resort is its dinner theater. The hotel says its medieval suppers, at which diners eat without benefit of utensils, are the most popular of the dinner theater presentations. Tour buses from Pittsburgh make weekend theater trips to Cambridge Springs, and other patrons come from Erie, a short distance away.

August 3

Towns, like people, offer first impressions. And just as with people, sometimes it's a positive first meeting, sometimes it's negative. At our breakfast stop on the day we cycled to Jamestown, New York, we rode into a town that gave off bad vibes. We'd cycled through several towns that gave us an uncomfortable feeling, but this town was the worst. We referred to these towns as the NO towns. As we entered, every sign had the word NO in it. NO parking! NO loitering! NO hunting! NO camping! In this particular town, there were NO signs we hadn't experienced. NO rest rooms! NO standing! NO skateboarding! The word NO dominated the signage. We quickly ate breakfast at a restaurant opposite a large cemetery (NO dogs), and then rapidly cycled out of this unwelcoming town.

As we traveled the northwestern corner of Pennsylvania, we knew we were in Amish country. We saw road signs warning us to expect horses and buggies in the road. But we didn't need the signs. We cycled around the evidence that horses had been on the road. It was a quiet Sunday, and there was no traffic. As we cycled in this

peaceful setting, we heard singing voices in the distance. Moments later we saw ten highly polished black buggies parked in front of a farmhouse. A worship service was being conducted. Not wanting to disturb the solemnity of the moment, we rode on some distance before stopping to get a photo of the farmhouse.

Later in the day we arrived in the town of Sugargrove. Clip-clop, clip-clop: We heard the approaching sound of horses as they pulled Amish families in their shiny black carriages. David hastily set up his camera. He wanted a good shot as the carriages approached. Click went his shutter. The first carriage slowed down. The Amish driver, nicely but firmly told David to cease his picture taking. As the long line of carriages passed, the Amish children smiled and waved to us. They were dressed in their Sunday best, black suits with straw hats for the boys, black dresses with white collars and headpieces for the girls. A scene from another time, the cortege made a pleasing sight.

In Sugargrove, we spoke with a father and son, both avid cyclists. They explained to us why the Amish gentleman had rebuked David for his picture-taking. The Amish do not like to be photographed. We learned from the Sugargrove natives that the Amish are good citizens; they pay town real estate taxes on their farms, but they do not use the public schools, preferring to educate their children themselves. We were told an Amish youngster's education terminates after the eighth grade. As an example of what good citizens the Amish are, the cyclist related how the previous year the firehouse needed a new roof. When the town could not find the funds to do the roofing, the Amish volunteered. In four days, the roof was complete.

We continued to chat with the father-son duo. They were interested in our trip, but we were more interested in discussing the Amish. From them we learned the Amish live without benefit of electricity or cars. We were curious. Do the Amish do all their traveling by horse and buggy? The father explained that automobile travel is permitted in someone else's vehicle. It is not unusual for a non-Amish person to take a group of Amish people to the store for shopping. Bus travel is also permitted. Our cycling friend related how he once hired an Amish gentleman to help him with a water problem. As the two of them worked side by side, he found the Amish gentleman to be conversant on all the issues of the day. Although radio and television are not part of the Amish culture, reading is. Reading by candlelight.

Shortly after we left Sugargrove, we crossed into New York State. As I called out, "We are now in our eleventh state," David corrected

me. "You are in your eleventh state. I am entering my twelfth state."
He reminded me again that Nebraska was included in his list of states.

State borders were memorable. Their crossing meant we were
getting closer to our destination. A new state often meant a change in
road surface, sometimes for the better, sometimes for the worse. New
York was a change for the better. At the state line a newly paved road
with a wide, smooth shoulder was there to greet us. But as we cycled
into Jamestown, we encountered a smooth, wide road still under
construction. We cycled the torn-up road for several miles. The afternoon
rush of city traffic, combined with the heavy road construction, made
us happy to find our motel.

August 4

For cyclists, the Amish horse and buggy warning signs along the road
are a welcome sight. Whenever one appears, the road ahead starts
winding or becomes hilly, obstructing the view of an automobile driver.
In these sections, the road has a wide, smooth shoulder to accommodate

the horse and buggy's safe
passage, and providing us
with some safe cycling.

It was drizzling as we
looked ahead and saw a
horse and buggy pull out
from a side road. Two
teenage boys wearing black
flat-brimmed hats sat erect
on the front seat. Their
horse moved along at a steady trotting gait. Our odometers indicated
they were traveling about ten miles per hour. The road was flat and
smooth, and we were moving along at a good pace. David looked at
me, I looked at David, and we nodded in agreement. We would pass
the buggy. Cautiously we moved to the left to warn the boys we were

about to pass. Was that a sly smile I detected on the young man's face? As we got alongside the carriage, we heard the boys cluck to their horse. Then there was an audible slap of the reins. The boys were urging the horse on. They wanted to race. If we were bold enough to pass, we'd better have the ability to keep up the pace. Hunkering down over our bicycles, we added more pressure with each turn of the crank and we never looked back. We pedaled furiously until we were out of earshot of the horse's gait. It was the first and only vehicle we passed on the trip.

We cycled through some Indian reservations, although no signs indicated we were on one. A quick look around confirmed it. The tax-free status of the reservations fosters businesses that draw customers from the surrounding area. Gas stations and smoke shops, more than needed for the local population, line the roads. Occasionally there is a bingo parlor. Each retail establishment offers goods at yesteryear prices. We compared the lively setting of this reservation to that of Pine Ridge, the Sioux reservation we cycled through in South Dakota, where we traveled for miles seeing only an occasional run-down home surrounded by junked cars. Later we learned that Pine Ridge reservation is one of the poorest areas in the United States.

For a few days in New York, we deviated from the Adventure Cycling maps and used our own routing. The change caused a major mishap. As we were biking toward Olean, we got lost. Seriously lost. We went seventeen miles in the wrong direction. David examined our detailed map of the area and concluded the map was incorrect. It showed our selected route continued, but we discovered it stopped abruptly. No signs along the way indicated we were on a dead-end road.

As we reviewed our mistake, we realized we should have picked up on some clues. Although the road surface was excellent, homes and businesses ceased after the first mile or two. There was no traffic. The only vehicle we saw was a state truck spraying herbicide along the side of the road. We noticed the solitude of the road, but the quality of the new pavement convinced us the road had to go somewhere. It did. The road terminated at the front entrance to a girls' summer camp.

Our only option was to retrace our route. After completing almost ten miles, we heard the sound of traffic. Lots of traffic. Route 17, one of the major highways across New York, was just across a farmer's field. Crossing it would save us seven miles of backtracking, so why not? Off we went, cycling across the recently mowed field. To reach the highway we had to climb up a steep embankment. We unpacked the bikes. Each trip up the embankment we threw another part of our gear over the guardrail onto the highway's breakdown lane. We laughed as we thought of what the motorists saw. First, some panniers. Then, a B.O.B. carrier. A bike. Another bike. Finally, two laughing cyclists jumped over the guardrail and quickly reassembled their vehicles. We waited for a break in the steady stream of traffic. Then we ran across the highway, crossed the median strip, and headed into the eastbound breakdown lane.

We cycled fast in the smooth breakdown lane. It was the sirens we heard first. Then a police car, its domed blue light flashing, passed us. The officer slowed up and pulled his car into the breakdown lane ahead of us. Was the police officer after us? Were we breaking the speed limit for bicycles? David, who had a history as a young man of getting speeding tickets, thought this was wonderful. A ticket for biking too fast! That would be a memento of the trip worth framing. Alas, speeding was not the problem. Route 17 is a limited-access road, and bikes are not allowed. Didn't we see the signs as we entered the highway? We didn't want to tell the officer how we'd entered the highway! We showed the officer our inaccurate map of the area and explained our mishap. He directed us to Alternate 17, a road designated for cyclists. As we rolled off the nearest exit, the police officer was there, verifying that we'd obeyed his directions.

While we waited out a thunderstorm at a McDonald's in Salamanca, David acquired another fan. The young man, returning to his car with sacks of McDonald goodies, saw our bikes resting against the building. He returned inside to find us. We were easy to find. We were the wet couple, devouring burgers and fries as puddles of water formed around us. As we consumed calories, the young man informed us he did some touring. He was now a family man, and lack of time prevented him from cycling long distances. He wanted to know about our route, our average daily mileage, and any problems we'd had. He couldn't get enough information. He wanted to trade places, to be cycling across the United States. He said it would be easy for him to step into the role: He already owned the same bike as David, a Trek 520 touring model; he cycled in the same shoes as David; he even wore the same cycling shirt as David. He was ready to go! As the young man continued to get his fill, listening to tales of our journey, we wondered about his family. We hoped they enjoyed cold burgers and fries.

August 5

Corning, New York presented a problem for us. The solitary country road we cycled from Olean kept joining busier roads. Finally, we were on a main highway. Trucks and cars whizzed by. It was frightening as the late afternoon traffic mounted. We pulled off, seeking an alternative route. A cyclist gave us some directions but either she was wrong or we improperly negotiated the route, because we arrived back at the same intersection from which we'd started. The directions we obtained from a construction worker also led nowhere. We could see Corning off in the distance, but we couldn't get there. Time was passing. David used his cell phone to call our inn and get directions. The innkeeper told us there was only one way to get into Corning—we had to take the major highway across the river. Two anxious cyclists joined the late afternoon rush of traffic on the highway into Corning. Our plans for an early arrival in Corning had been thwarted. We wanted to visit the Steuben Glass factory but we arrived too late, and both of us were disappointed. However, Corning offered us a charming place to stay, the Rosewood Inn.

One of the innkeepers, Suzanne Sanders, wearing a long flowing skirt, a dried rose pinned to the collar of her blouse, was standing in the road waiting for us. She wanted to make sure we'd correctly followed her directions. The tangy lemonade and sweet cookies Suzanne laid out for us were a fine conclusion to a long cycling day. As we consumed the goodies, we learned that she and her husband, Stewart, had left the stressful world of corporate life to run the Rosewood Inn. Stewart's health problems were an incentive to seek the relaxed setting of an inn. Stewart Sanders relaxes further by baking, and we needed to eat. It was a great combination.

August 6

We awoke to a perfect day. High thin clouds, dry air, light northwesterly winds, blue skies, temperatures in the sixties—everything about the day said "welcome." We omitted our pre-breakfast start because we needed to sample Stewart's baking talents at breakfast. As we sat around the large communal table, we conversed with other guests of the inn. One couple informed us they cycled, frequently doing long rides around their home in eastern Virginia. The gentleman was interested in our bikes and had given them a once over as they leaned against the front porch. Neither of us could answer his questions about gear ratios and packing hubs. All we can do on a bicycle are basic repairs.

David is not mechanically minded. He doesn't mind admitting that to friends, but it's different with strangers. It must be a male thing. Males are supposed to know about their sports equipment, whether it be skis, bikes, cars or boats. What David knows about his equipment comes from the salespeople who sell it to him. When the gentleman at the Rosewood Inn started questioning us about our bikes I could see David grow tense. His jaw tightened. He wanted the conversation to shift to any topic other than bikes—to the wonderful breakfast we were enjoying, to our cross-country ride. David would have done anything to disguise his ineptitude as a bike mechanic. Fortunately, the other breakfast guests were not interested in cycling and were happy to have the conversation shift to the local baseball team, whose game some guests had attended the previous evening.

We took our first break of the day in Watkins Glen, about thirty miles north of Corning. We were fortunate our trip didn't put us there later in the week. Signs along the road read, "Welcome Race Fans." NASCAR races at the Glen were scheduled for the weekend, and some fans were already making their way to the famous track. From our earlier years when we lived in the auto racing capital of the U. S.— Daytona Beach, Florida—we knew about car racing fans. After races at the Daytona Beach Speedway were over, enthusiastic fans often tested their driving skills on nearby roads. We didn't want to be in the area as fans attempted fast straight-aways and tight turns on surrounding highways.

The remainder of the day offered some of the most beautiful cycling of the trip. We climbed out of Watkins Glen to the east ridge of Seneca Lake, one of New York's Finger Lakes. The lake, off our left side, was never out of sight. Vineyards line the lake, and we stopped frequently to take photos. Roadside farm stands offered fresh fruit for snacking. At lunchtime we stopped at Wagner Vineyards. Their outdoor café, overlooking Seneca Lake, was an idyllic setting for a delicious lunch on a perfect cycling day.

Our accommodations in Geneva were at Belhurst Castle, an 1890 brick mansion converted into an inn. As we sat relaxing, enjoying the lakeside grounds, a staff person called us to the phone. We knew we were about to receive bad news. Friends and family had our daily itinerary, but we did not communicate by phone. Cards and letters from friends were mailed to us. E-mail was sent and received several times a week. Whatever phone calls we made were on layover days. But as soon as David heard our friend Bud's voice on the phone, we knew.

Don, a dear friend of ours, was struggling with recurring cancer. Bud informed us Don had suffered a seizure and had been hospitalized.

His gallant fight was coming to an end. Don did not want us informed of his condition. But Bud thought otherwise. He was correct.

We heard our call to dinner in the elegant Belhurst Castle without enthusiasm. We ate because we had to eat. We could not appreciate the creatively prepared food. We sat muddled within our thoughts. After dinner we separated, each of us seeking the peacefulness of the grounds overlooking the moon-swept lake. As I wandered, an older couple approached me and told me they had seen us eating lunch at the Wagner Vineyards. I was not in the mood to discuss our journey. I quickly blurted out how we'd learned that evening of our friend's seizure. The couple startled me back into reality. "It is something you'll have to get used to", they said. "This is news you'll experience with greater frequency as you age."

As we cycled the United States, we did not feel our age. We were realizing a long-held dream. We were on a trip we would never forget. Meanwhile, a friend our age was embarking on his final journey. Mentally I dedicated the remainder of our cross-country trip to Don.

August 7

As we left Geneva for our destination on Lake Ontario, near Pulaski, we spent part of the morning crossing over and biking beside sections of the Erie Canal. The extensive canal system was unknown to us. At one of the locks we stopped to chat with the operator. He informed us the canal system covers more than five hundred miles and contains fifty-seven locks. The system is maintained solely for pleasure boats with the state keeping the system open from May to October. From brochures the lock operator gave us, we learned many entrepreneurs are developing tours along the canals. Companies offer self-piloted houseboats that, if you believe the brochures, have every amenity, including air-conditioning. Seneca Falls, a picturesque town on the canal system, is gearing up for the ever-increasing canal traffic. We noticed plenty of

moorings, numerous stores to service the boaters, and an abundance
of inns for those who want accommodations off the water.

We reached Oswego,
a city on Lake Ontario,
around two o'clock in the
afternoon. On our way out
of town, we missed a turn
and discovered we were on
the wrong road. Why
retrace the route? How lost
could we get if we
paralleled the lake? Our
accommodations were directly on Lake Ontario.

Our selected road was perfect: no traffic, good surface. We
occasionally lost sight of the lake, but the sun stayed to our left, indicating
we were heading north. After about twenty miles we saw the dreaded
sign, "Road Closed." A heavy equipment crane, holding aloft a large
piece of piping, filled the streambed. A new bridge was being constructed.
We asked the crane operator about a detour. As soon as he said "twenty
miles back," we knew we would find an alternative solution to retracing
our route. The day was rapidly closing. David hiked along the stream
and found a place where, if we stepped from rock to rock, we could
cross. We unpacked our bikes. Jointly we carried each piece of cargo
through the woods and set it down. Piece by piece we carried our gear
across the stream and then up a steep hill covered with trees and shrubs.
It was a time-consuming operation, about an hour from start to finish.
We finally got our bikes and gear to the other side, a distance of no
more that fifty feet from our starting point. Once we reassembled our
loads, we celebrated by sharing a high five as we leaned against a Road
Closed sign barring the traffic on the opposite shore. We had beaten
another Road Closed sign!

Our arrival at Rainbow Shores Motel on Lake Ontario was after six o'clock. The difficulty of the day melted away as we sat on the motel's large dining deck sipping beer and taking in the lakeside view. By now we took our mishaps as a matter of course and laughed them off. However, we were always pleased when we resolved them.

As we dined on steak, the motel's well trained dog waited patiently for a meal. Could we resist those dark brown eyes? No other diners could. Finally we succumbed and offered her bits of meat. But, she did not get one morsel of my rich chocolate brownie sundae.

A hushed crowd sat on Rainbow Shores' deck watching the sun sink over Lake Ontario. The beauty of the sunset required concentration, because each minute brought a change in coloration, from pale pink to vibrant red. As the final red glow disappeared, night fell and we returned to our room. The sound of the waves of Lake Ontario slapping the shore lulled us to sleep.

August 8

As we hit the road for our ride to Old Forge, a town centered in the Adirondack Mountains, we encountered tire problems. It was difficult to believe, but it was our first tire problem since Oregon. The first flat tire occurred shortly after we started cycling. It was on my rear wheel (the more difficult tire to change because of the chain and gearing) and was made more cumbersome by my having the B.O.B. attached, needing to first disengage the carrier from the rear hub. The second flat occurred shortly after the first as we started climbing a mountain. What was the matter? David is an experienced tire changer! He seldom pinches a tube when he changes a tire. We would never make Old Forge at the rate we were destroying tubes. Finally, on the third flat, we carefully inspected the interior of the rear tire. It took some time to find the sliver of metal, no thicker than a hair, lodged in my rear tire. The problem was solved. We relaxed, knowing tube number four was going to go the distance.

Whenever we cycled into a town during early morning hours, we could always spot the breakfast café. Cars and trucks were parked in front of what we dubbed the local Breakfast Club. Most of the Breakfast Clubs open by 5:30 A.M., and none later than 6:00. As patrons enter, "*Good Morning*"s and "*How you doin'?*"s spread around the room. Many customers don't order: The "usual" is automatically delivered. As outsiders in these tightly knit groups of townspeople, we needed menus to decide on our breakfast choices. We often overheard locals discussing crops, the weather, and problematic neighbors. A morning pub is what a Breakfast Club is.

A Friday afternoon in summer was not a good time to be cycling into the Adirondack region. On the main route that leads into Old Forge, we discovered the popularity of the mountainous region. No Vacancy signs hung from motels. The cities of Utica and Rome, not too far south of Old Forge, empty out every summer weekend, and the steady stream of traffic was evidence of the exodus.

Next to tourism, forestry is the mainstay of the Adirondack region's economy. At our lunch break in Boonville, we chatted with the garrulous owner of a health food store. On his own lunch break, he was happy to delay his return to the store by engaging us in conversation. He said the biggest event of the year—the annual woodsmen's competition—was scheduled for the weekend. From all around the United States loggers would come to compete in events, from wood chopping to maneuvering heavy logging equipment. For my benefit he added there are many events for women loggers. He said women, who have good fine motor skills, are adept at maneuvering large logging equipment, which require precision driving.

At the Sunset Motel in Old Forge, David acquired yet another fan. He was one of the owners of the motel. When making the reservation, I had mentioned we would be arriving on bikes. As we pulled in, the owner was waiting for us. While unloading our bikes, David answered his questions: How long did it take to plan the trip?

What kind of tires work best? How do the panniers change your cycling style? He couldn't get enough.

Several years ago, he told us, he got into cycling as a way to control his weight. He rode daily, weather permitting. He wintered in Florida and continued his cycling there. Each year he rode six thousand miles! He was so happy to have cyclists to talk to that he invited David to inspect his expensive bicycle, secure on a rack in the garage. No sooner was the invitation offered than I could feel David growing tense again. I could read his thoughts. "Oh, no, not a bicycle gear-head. All I want to do is shower and have a beer."

A half hour later David returned to the room. His face was relaxed, so I knew his encounter with the motel owner had gone well.

As we crossed the country we developed a bad habit. We became TV junkies. As soon as we entered our room for the night, we rushed to turn on the TV. It was not to view a sitcom or watch CNN. We needed to catch the latest updates from the Weather Channel. We likened this to asking drivers about the terrain of the roads ahead. No matter what they told us, we cycled on. It was the same with weather. We absorbed all the information the Weather Channel offered. Possible low-pressure system? High-pressure system? Wind? Thunderstorms likely? We don't know why we became weather addicts because none of the news made any difference to us. Like the U.S. Postal Service, we forged ahead in all weather.

August 9

As we prepared to leave Old Forge for Saranac Lake at 5:30 A.M., Mr. Motel Owner, avid cyclist, was there to see us off. He described the first part of our route, which was his daily ride. We, too, would have made it a daily ride if we lived in the area. The route was beautiful. We'd never seen so many lakes. One flowed into another. Seldom were we out of sight of water. In the Fulton Chain, lakes are numbered, rather than named. We cycled by the Fourth, Fifth, Sixth, and Seventh Lakes.

The deer living around the town of Old Forge are afraid of nothing, bikes included. When I first encountered one, I thought it was a statue. It should have been an ornament on someone's lawn, not in the middle of the road. My excitement at seeing so many deer in our path soon abated as we found ourselves maneuvering our bikes around them. The deer barely noticed us as they moved from one side of the road to the other devouring expensive shrubbery. We wondered how these domesticated deer fared during hunting season. Did they take up protective residence in the summer camps that line the lakes?

Off to the right we heard a rustling through the trees. We quickly looked in the direction of the noise. Scurrying as fast as he could, a black bear moved away from us. In the Adirondacks the black bear population is plentiful, and from the number of fenced-in, locked trash receptacles we saw, they must know where to find a meal.

We pulled alongside Hotel Saranac late in the day. Eight cycling days had passed since our last day off, and we were looking forward to a layover day. It would be our last of the trip. Our next day off the bikes would indicate the trip was over.

The town of Saranac Lake sits nestled among several lakes. On an early evening stroll we saw a storefront poster advertising, in bold lettering, the outstanding statistics of the quaint town. Saranac Lake was voted the number one small town in New York State and the number eleventh small town in the United States. Nowhere was it posted who compiled Saranac Lake's impressive statistics, but as we walked around the town we found it charming and worthy of recognition.

On our way back to the hotel, we heard rock music filling the air. Saranac Lake is a popular location for weddings, and our hotel was hosting one. The boisterous, happy wedding party was enjoying the warm summer evening, celebrating in the hotel's second-floor banquet room and on its outdoor patio. The next morning we were glad we'd stored our bikes inside. Lining the sidewalk below the patio were broken pots of geraniums, dropped to the ground by exuberant, if irresponsible, wedding guests.

Before we stored our bikes for the night, we inspected them. We washed off the daily grime that had collected on their frames, and we lubricated the chains. A nightly task for David was to check the pressure in our tires. This was something new for him. For years David has told me I have a fetish. Prior to starting any bike ride, I pumped up my tires, explaining, "Inflated tires roll better."

David retorted, "A few pounds one way or the other won't make any difference."

When we had tire problems back in Oregon, David purchased a pressure gauge—a device that measures a tire's air pressure. This simple tool started David doing nightly checks. If a tire was low by just five pounds, he inflated it. Was it the gauge that prompted the nightly checks, or did he finally realize that inflated tires roll better? Whatever the reason, David became a convert and we both had fully inflated tires for the entire trip.

August 10

We spent our layover day reading weekly news magazines in a park next to Lake Flower. As the afternoon drew to a close, we rented a small motorboat to do some sightseeing. We are not boat-savvy people. If the boat's motor died, we weren't sure we could restart it. For that reason neither of us wanted to negotiate any of the locks connecting the lakes. We stayed in the lakes we could reach without entering a lock. As we motored along, we marveled at the beauty of the Adirondack Mountains. They are like no other mountains we've ever seen. The peaks appear to overlap and intersect one another, giving an overall effect of undulating waves. It was a striking image in the soft light of the setting sun.

We concluded our layover day in the Adirondacks agreeing we wanted to return. The mountainous region is close to our home, yet this was our first visit. The beauty of the area overwhelmed us, and we were pleased to learn large areas of it are protected from development—over two and a half million acres designated as "forever wild". We vowed to return to this land of so many lakes that they're numbered, not named!

Chapter 10

Home Again

Saranac Lake, New York, to	Miles	Elevation Gain (ft.)
Aug 11	Middlebury, Vermont	95	4,650
Aug 12	Lyme, New Hampshire	74	4,550
Aug 13	Conway, New Hampshire	82	4,880
Aug 14	Newcastle, Maine	129	6,350
Aug 15	Camden, Maine	33	1,760
Aug 16	Bar Harbor, Maine	76	3,410

MILEAGE: 489 / ELEVATION GAIN: 25,600 FEET

Total Mileage: 4,622
Total Elevation Gain: 158,440 feet

August 11

David and I had mixed feelings as we started our last week of cycling. One part of us wanted to return to the "real world," and the other part wanted to keep the journey going. We were anxious to see family and friends. I wanted to check the tomato plants I'd put in before leaving home. But we knew we would miss the adventure of our cycling trip. Each day was different. Rain, hills, flat tires, "Road Closed" signs—how would each day unfold?

We left Saranac Lake at dawn to cycle to the Winter Olympics town of Lake Placid. We needed breakfast, but there are no early morning cafés in Lake Placid, because it is tourist country! Tourists don't breakfast at 5:30 A.M. So we parked our bikes outside a café, strolling the area close by, waiting for the restaurant to open.

Across the street was the Olympic skating arena where the U.S. men's 1980 ice hockey team beat the formidable and favored Russians

in the semi-finals and then went on to win the gold medal. We watched the history-making game in a bar in Vermont. We cheered as Massachusetts native, Mike Erusioni, scored the game-winning goal, upsetting the Russians 4 to 3. At the final buzzer the patrons in the bar shouted, "We won! We won! We beat the Russians!" Soon everyone was standing on chairs cheering and waving small United States flags. We remembered that moment as we waited for breakfast in Lake Placid.

There is a waitress in Lake Placid I want to put on a bicycle. I want her to cycle the fourteen miles from Lake Placid to Keene, New York. After that she will never deceive another cyclist. When we inquired about the terrain of the road to Keene, she emphatically responded, "Oh, it's a gradual downhill." She was remembering the last five miles into Keene, which indeed are downhill. The first nine are not. We passed Olympic ski jumps, bobsled runs, and ski slopes. We climbed the mountains that offer these Olympic sports. We were in good enough shape not to let the hills bother us, but we'd counted on making good time. It was another reminder to us: never, never, never ask an automobile driver about terrain. Ask cyclists, skateboarders, runners, Rollerbladers, or walkers, but not drivers!

As we rode past a swampy area on our way to Ticonderoga, New York, I watched a large bird circle overhead. I followed it as it perched on a dead tree. As soon as I saw its red-crested head, I knew it had to be a Pileated Woodpecker. What a find! I had never seen one before. I yelled to David. He didn't hear me and rode on. I had to stop to look at the large bird, the model for the cartoon character Woody Woodpecker. David could wait for me.

On our route into Middlebury, we'd see large aircraft as they continued their climb out of Boston's Logan Airport, less than two hundred miles to the southeast, on their way to the west coast. It was a jet route we were familiar with—one we took every time we visited our daughter Stephanie in California. As we watched the jets reach their assigned altitude we couldn't help thinking how in six hours the passengers of those planes would be arriving on the west coast and how it had taken us eight weeks of cycling to get here.

I must confess, we did not cycle every mile of our cross-country trip. In Ticonderoga we took a ferry across Lake Champlain. Rolling our bikes off the ferry, we entered hill country—Vermont. Our introduction was immediate as we made our way to Middlebury. The hills didn't cease until we coasted past the scenic campus of Middlebury College to enter the center of town.

August 12

It took us one day to cross Vermont. As we crossed the state from west to east, we were again reminded why we love Vermont, our second home. For years we've owned a vacation home in Vermont's north-ern Green Mountains.

Many of the roads we cycled were familiar to us—they felt like old friends. We climbed steep hills, and we were rewarded with spectacular, though familiar, sights: small, quaint towns with spired white churches; lush, green valley fields stocked with dairy cows; treed mountains bearing thick, summer foliage; cold rushing streams. We were happy to be back home.

Our first significant climb was Middlebury Gap. It is the least steep of the four gaps—Middlebury, Brandon, Appalachian, and Lincoln— that cross the center of the Green Mountain range. As we climbed the gap, we passed the Mount Breadloaf campus of Middlebury College. We didn't know the academic scope of the campus, but we thought students who got to spend time in the lush mountain setting were fortunate. Dark green Adirondack chairs, picturesquely scattered in a meadow overlooking Mount Breadloaf, appeared inviting. As I cycled by, I daydreamed about being nestled in one of those chairs, a favorite book in my lap, sipping hot coffee and viewing the idyllic setting of the meadow.

Middlebury Ski Bowl is near the summit of the gap, so when we cycled past the ski area, we knew we were about to enjoy a long downhill. Our descent took us into the town of Hancock, where we joined Route 100, a cyclist's dream road. Travel magazines often rate Route 100 as the most scenic road in Vermont. On this clear, cool, summer day, we had to concur. We rode through a narrow valley, bordered by steep mountains, and listened to the White River rush along beside us.

Decisions, decisions. Our minds, on vacation for so long, needed more time. Our luncheon stop was at the Sugar House in Royalton. The long list of maple desserts was impressive, but we narrowed the field. Maple pecan pie or maple walnut ice cream? Finally we made a decision: pie for me, ice cream for David, with promises of sample tastes.

It was on the afternoon we cycled across Vermont that we started having a new regard for the word hill. *Pass* and *gap* are words we've always respected. They indicate what to expect: tough, steep, long climbs. As we started up Tucker Hill, a climb we'd never done, we kept saying to each other, "This can't go on much longer. It's only a hill." The road kept going up. After an hour of tough cycling, we reached the top and took a well-deserved break. I asked, "Are you sure that was described as a hill?"

Shortly afterward, we climbed Thetford Hill, another Vermont challenge, one we'd done before but didn't recall its steepness. At the summit of Thetford Hill, we jointly announced that the word *hill* had officially gained our respect. It was now a descriptive word we would not take lightly!

Late in the afternoon we crossed the Connecticut River, the dividing line between Vermont and New Hampshire, and made the short run into Lyme. The setting of Lyme is what comes to mind when you think of a New England village. Displayed in the large green in the town center are war memorials from the Civil War through the Vietnam era. Large white colonial houses, their shutters painted black, surround the green. On our way around the town green, we saw our accommodations for the evening, the Alden Country Inn.

As we were shown to our room, the staff person told us the dining room of the inn was highly rated, although he didn't tell us who had done the rating. We didn't know at the time we were speaking to the owner and chef. He told us that tonight they had a special on the menu: fresh oysters and clams from Maine. We were thrilled. Fresh Atlantic seafood! It was further evidence we were getting closer to our destination. We stuffed ourselves with fried oysters and raw clams and reviewed our remaining itinerary. The next day we would cross New Hampshire. Then it was just Maine, our last state.

It was strange how we needed visible signs, such as Maine shellfish on a menu, to remind us we were closing in on the finish. Our days had taken on a certain tempo. Up at dawn, cycling during the day, and relaxing at the close of the day. It didn't seem real to us that we were close to Bar Harbor, our last stop. Being served Maine oysters and clams helped us settle into that reality.

August 13

As we stepped outside at 5:30 A.M. to start our ride we felt the first drops of rain. The Weather Channel had predicted a day of heavy rain in northern New England. We hoped the forecast was wrong. After all, we were in New England, the region people refer to when they say, "If you don't like the weather, just wait a minute." We thought of a weather forecaster we'd met in Florida who, when discovering we came from New England, told us, "You are so lucky. You have weather!" Today we would have been happy not to have weather.

The forecasters were correct. A nor'easter, delivering pelting rain, started early and continued throughout the day. It wasn't long before we—and our gear—were soaked. On the climbs, we sweated. On the downhills, we froze. Water ran off our noses. Our protective eyewear was steamed up. As I passed a road crew making emergency repairs, they asked me, "Are you crazy?" I nodded my head. I managed the first long climb by thinking of our terminally ill friend, Don. As uncomfortable as we were, the day would pass. Tomorrow was another day. How many tomorrows did Don have?

We pulled into North Woodstock, New Hampshire, for a late breakfast and shivered as we ate. Puddles of water settled around us. The restaurant patrons stared at us as we devoured our large breakfasts.

As we left the restaurant, the rain came down harder. We stood under the eaves, looking at the street, which was more like a river than a road. But we had no options. Reluctantly, we returned to our bikes. Before starting our second climb, the Kancamagus Highway, we knew we needed more waterproofing. We tried to buy ponchos. Sold out. We decided would make our own ponchos. Soon we were under a store's sale tent cutting holes in large trash bags with David's Swiss army knife. We giggled as we slipped on our homemade ponchos. We were definitely making a new fashion statement for cyclists. For a short time, the trash bag layer worked. But it was a drenching rain. Nothing would stay dry.

Slowly we climbed the Kancamagus Highway, one of the passes through the White Mountains. Traffic was heavy. Tourists were heading to North Conway, on the eastern side. Why? To do what tourists do on rainy days: Shop at the discount outlet stores in North Conway.

The 23 mile downhill into Conway was the most dangerous cycling of the trip. Rain swept the road in sheets. We rode with our brakes on to slow us down on the slick surface. By the time we reached Conway, on the eastern side, I was cold and numb. I informed David I couldn't continue, because I was too tired and my body was shaking. David tried to change my mind, saying it was only thirty more miles. I stood by my decision.

"Remember, David, we are a team. One quits, the other quits."

We stopped at eighty-two miles. We didn't make it to our destination, which was Waterford, Maine.

We were lucky to find a motel in Conway with a room available because rained-out campers traipsed into town as well. It was an embarrassing check-in; David and I left puddles of water on the clean rug. Within minutes of getting to our room, I struggled out of my wet clothing to soak in a hot tub.

A necessary piece of equipment for a touring cyclist is a hair dryer. It helps make difficult hair manageable, but it also serves another function: It dries out cycling shoes. Nothing is more uncomfortable than stepping into squishy, wet shoes. We also used the blow dryer on our wet bike saddles. We were sure the guests in the adjoining rooms thought the long-haired Rapunzel was in the next room—the dryer was on for hours.

As darkness set in, the rain stopped. It took both of us to lug all our water-soaked clothing to the Laundromat, which was filled to capacity. Long lines formed at the dryers. Campers shared our problem. Their gear was also soaked.

Tired and hungry, we walked the streets of Conway with our freshly dried clothes. Soon we found respite at the Alpenglow, a small, friendly bistro. The food was good and plentiful, and we started to revive. Our dinner conversation centered on how our stay in Conway was just the second time we hadn't made our planned destination. Our first had occurred back in Oregon, when we'd had tire problems. We left the restaurant carrying our laundry bag between us to return to our motel for the best restorer of all—sleep.

We felt bad that we didn't make it to our destination. Waiting for us at the Waterford Inn, our planned stop, was Andrew, a cycling friend who would ride with us the last three days of the trip.

August 14

Because we had an extra thirty miles to cycle, we were on the road before sunrise, even though we needed more sleep. But as we covered the challenging miles, we realized our decision to quit early the day before was a wise one. Darkness would have settled in before we reached Waterford and that combined with the rain would have made the ride impossible.

Eager and excited to be biking, Andrew, twenty years our junior, was waiting for us at the general store in Waterford. His enthusiasm for being on the road showed. He rushed up hills and at the top would balance his bright yellow mountain bike, Trek spelled out in large red lettering along the crossbar, watching us as we made our slower ascent. Andrew's bike was the sleekest, fastest-looking bicycle we'd ever seen. It had front and rear shocks and a seat with no post, just suspended from the crossbar. For this trip Andrew had removed the mountain biking tires and replaced them with road tires. That did nothing to change the hot rod appearance. No awkward-looking panniers for Andrew, either. Attached to a suspended rack below his seat was a small knapsack, held in place with bungee cords. It carried enough for three days on the road.

Most roads in Maine are terrible for cyclists, because they have no shoulder. Whenever we cycled up a hill, cars usually stayed behind us until we'd reached the top. There the driver could get a clear view of what was ahead. Most drivers gave us the time and space required. However, we encountered an irate passenger. The man's wife was driving, and their two young children were in the backseat. As the car slowed on the hill behind David and Andrew, the man stretched himself out the window, shook his fist, and shouted, "Get the fuck off the road!" I was just starting the short, steep climb, so I saw it all. The wife, embarrassed, tried to stop her husband. I hollered, "Nice language for children!" He returned to the car.

Late in the morning we met a group of cyclists— three young women, two of whom were sisters, and a young man. They were completing Adventure Cycling's northern route. We all excitedly related some of our experiences of the past nine weeks. They talked about fighting severe headwinds as they crossed upper Michigan, something we'd avoided on our route. We spoke about cycling through yesterday's heavy rains. One of the women asked, "Why would you do that? We started out but as soon the rain got heavy, we found a motel and holed up for the day, playing cards and watching TV."

"We are on a set itinerary, staying in motels every night," replied David.

"You aren't doing any camping?" asked another of the women.

"No, we are too old for that," David answered. "A good night's sleep is what allows us to cycle day after day."

"We do half and half," said the young man. "After a night or two in a campground we need a bath and a good night's sleep, so we stay in a motel. It's worked out well. I'm glad we weren't cycling with you yesterday. That was the worst weather we've seen on the trip."

We agreed. After almost nine weeks on the road, that unrelenting downpour was the worst weather we'd cycled in.

The group was trying to slow their pace. A big party was scheduled for their arrival in Bar Harbor, and they didn't want to arrive early, ruining the plans of their friends and family.

As the four of them huddled over a map, making a decision about which road to take, we said "Good-bye. Good-luck" and rode on. The long hill that led us into Turner, Maine, provided some glorious views, but we discovered it was not the correct route. Again we'd made a routing error and added miles to the day.

The closer we got to the Maine coast, the more frequent and steep the hills got. The terrain brought me close to tears. Down a hill, only to go up a hill. There were no flat sections, and the hills continued for miles. I couldn't let the hills beat me. I cursed under my breath and played mind games. Andrew, his legs fresh and his enthusiasm unbounded, cheered us on. "Come on, guys. You've biked across the country. You can make the hills."

All of us shouted with joy when we rolled into Newcastle just as the sun was starting to set. Andrew was ecstatic. If he cycled one more mile, he would complete his first century ride. While David and I limped ahead to our destination, Andrew spun his wheels for another mile.

Darkness was settling in as we pulled into the driveway of the Newcastle Inn. There was no time to relax. The innkeeper told us we had half an hour to get ourselves to the dining room if we wanted dinner. Quick showers. Clothes thrown on. We were ordering food within twenty-five minutes of our arrival. No cyclist could go without food after the strenuous day we'd had. When David finished compiling his numbers, he stated we had done the second most difficult day of the trip, 129 miles and 6,350 feet of elevation gain. No wonder I was so exhausted!

August 15

When we awoke at the Newcastle Inn, I experienced a new feeling. For the first time since starting the trip, I didn't want to bike. The thought of getting on my bike was repulsive. I needed to rest. I wanted to linger on the deck of the Newcastle Inn sipping coffee. I longed to chat with people. I craved to go shopping. I wanted to be reading a newspaper. I was willing to do anything but ride my bike. My body was reacting to the two previous tough days of cycling. Loud and clear it was screaming, "Enough!"

Our planned ride for the day was to Camden, a mere thirty-three miles north. I couldn't get over the irony of it: The shortest day of the entire trip, and I didn't want to do it. I had to put my mind to work. What's thirty-three miles? That's shorter than most training rides. Just do it. I fought with myself. I mounted my bike and moved the pedals. I don't think I looked up until we rounded a corner and lovely Camden Harbor, filled with boats of all sizes and color, greeted us.

Summer crowds mingled in the streets of Camden. We lunched at an outdoor seafood café overlooking Camden's busy harbor. It was a sparkling, clear day. Bright sails floated by. Wonderful seaside smells filled the air. We had reached the Atlantic Ocean. One more day and we would be in Bar Harbor.

In Camden, we stayed at the beautiful Norumbega Inn, which sits high above the harbor. When I'd made the reservation in January and was quoted the price, I responded, "But we just want to stay one night." The staff person assured me that was the nightly price.

We rode our bikes into the inn's circular drive, where our Trek 520s were company to a long line of expensive cars. Andrew rode on to spend the night with friends in Belfast, Maine. As we stepped into our oceanview room, I knew David had chosen a special place for us to spend our last night on the road. From our spot high above Camden Harbor, we saw hundreds of boats maneuver their way about, to and from the sea: windjammers, with their tall masts and complex sets of sails; smaller boats with colorful spinnakers ballooning out, catching the wind; fishing boats; tourist boats; lobster boats—all were part of the moving picture. It was difficult to take our eyes off the large picture window, but when we looked around our room, we got another equally pleasurable view. Our room was luxurious. White, pink, and mauve fabrics covered the bed and the cushions of white wicker chairs. Freshly arranged flowers were beside our bed. A sherry-filled crystal decanter with matching glasses had been placed on a table for our use. No comfort had been overlooked. As I stepped into the bathroom, lined with thick, plush towels, I realized the extent of the luxury provided by the innkeeper: The toilet seat, to guarantee its sanitary condition, was circled with a wide pink satin ribbon, a large bow gracing the center. We slept the afternoon away in that luxurious seaside setting.

At dinner we discussed how the next day was day number sixty-three. Our final day on the road. We both had a bittersweet feeling about ending the trip. I recollected for David a remark he had made as we embarked on the trip back in Astoria, Oregon. He said, "Melissa, this a sad day!" When I questioned the meaning of his remark, he responded, "It's sad because we no longer have this day to look forward to." How true! The actual doing of the trip was an incredible experience, but planning the trip, anticipating the trip, and training for the trip were also wonderful. For a year this bike trip had been the central focus of our lives. We'd spent the entire year living our itinerary in our minds. Not a day went by that we didn't refer to the large United States map with our cross-country route penciled in. That part of our life would end tomorrow.

August 16

Day sixty-three. We were starting our last day on the road. A misty drizzle filled the air and visibility was poor. Traffic was light as we headed to Belfast to meet Andrew. Together we rode along the Maine coast, the fog obscuring our view of the Atlantic Ocean, just off our right shoulders. At breakfast our excitement started to build. Andrew kept reminding us what we would be accomplishing that day. He couldn't keep still. He kept smiling and saying, "I can't believe it! You guys are awesome!" He was so happy to be part of our trip.

Summer traffic was building. In Ellsworth, gateway to Bar Harbor and Acadia National Park, the sun came out. With it, humidity arrived. We were closing in, and nothing could deter us! Not the roads torn up by construction. Not the humidity. Not the steady stream of traffic. Nothing! We picked up the pace. We were racing to the finish. At two o'clock we passed the road sign "Entering Bar Harbor." We coasted into our hotel parking lot, large smiles across our sweaty faces.

We dismounted our bikes and shared a hard "high five," our final one of the trip. Our traditional daily closure was over.

"Well done, David."

"Well done, Melissa."

Andrew joined in the celebration, giving us high fives, saying "Way to go, guys! Nice job! Glad I could join you."

Before any celebrating, we had a job to do. We unloaded our gear and biked to the shore of the Atlantic Ocean. The streets of Bar Harbor were filled with summer tourists. We walked down a boat ramp and dipped our front wheels into the icy Atlantic waters, completing the cross-country tradition: rear wheels in the Pacific Ocean, front wheels in the Atlantic Ocean.

We had done it! We had crossed fourteen states. Our odometers read 4,622 miles. Our trip of a lifetime was over. But what a trip!

Our family was in Bar Harbor to welcome us. It was good to see them. As requested, they drove an extra car to Maine. After nine weeks

on the road, with only our bikes for transportation, we were going to
need a car to get home.

When we went to our room, we found chilled champagne,
bouquets of flowers, and a bottle of lovely French wine—all sent by
friends and family. There were messages of congratulations.

Whoa! We needed time to adjust, to have reality sink in. We were
finished! We'd made it to Bar Harbor! After nine weeks on the road,
we were done. No more hills to climb. No more cycling before sunrise.
No more hours in the Laundromat. No more dipping tired feet in cold,
rushing streams. No more rides in the rain. No more celebratory beers
at the end of a hard day. But it was time. It was time to return to a
different life.

It was a large, happy group that dined that evening at Testa's,
a restaurant located on Bar Harbor's main thoroughfare, on lobster,
steamed clams, corn-on-the-cob, and fresh raspberry pie. As we ate,
our family kept telling us they had a surprise waiting for us at home—
something we would cherish forever. "What is it?" I kept asking.

"OK," said our daughter Jenny, relenting. "We had the map you
and Dad worked on all year—the one that has your itinerary on it—matted
and framed. Can't wait for you to see it. It's beautiful. We even had a small
plaque saying 'Norton Cross Country Bike Trip' put on the frame."

David and I thanked our daughters and their husbands. What
a perfect gift—our year of planning, our summer of cycling—saved for
future referencing and reminiscing.

The next day as David and I drove home to Massachusetts, our
bikes secure in the rooftop rack, we talked about our summer. No longer
would it be just the two of us coping with the challenges of each day.
Our lives would return to something else: Responsibilities at work. Busy
schedules. But nothing could take away the memory of a summer just
the two of us spent on the road.

As weeks and months passed and we reminisced about the trip,
we often recalled the words of a German tourist we'd encountered the

first week of the trip. As we climbed a steep hill in Oregon, we passed the tourist, standing beside his car in a scenic turnout, photographing the valley below. As we rode by, he said in broken English "Ja, Ja, gut vay to go! Biking fun. You lucky."

I smiled at him. Not having enough breath to bike and converse, I blurted out as loud as I could, "Wunderbar!"

The tourist's eyes lit up and his mouth moved into a large grin. With his arms outstretched, his body shaking with enthusiasm, he shouted, "Ja! Ja! Ja! Wunderbar! Wunderbar!" He expressed so eloquently our feelings about our shared cross-country cycling trip. It truly was wonderful, wonderful!

Afterword

The most frequently asked question we received after returning home was, "What part of the trip did you like best?" Truthfully, we couldn't answer. Yes, there are sections of the country that are more beautiful than others. But for us, the trip was like creating a large oil painting. Each day we added another brush stroke to the canvas. Some days the strokes were wide, bold, and filled with color. Other days the strokes were soft and delicate. But each day contributed to the journey. Our painting wasn't complete until we finished the entire trip from Oregon to Maine.

To those who questioned what parts of the country we found most beautiful, we hesitated to give an answer. Conditions on a particular day made a difference. On a previous trip, we had fallen in love with Big Hole Valley in Montana. We looked forward to viewing the snow-capped Bitterroot Range, the awkward-looking beaverslides that catapult hay into piles, and the miles of split-rail fencing. We never saw any of it. Our ride through Big Hole Valley was on a cold, rainy, low-visibility day. In contrast, our ride along the Lochsa River, in Idaho, was on a cloudless, sunny day. The cool mist created by the river raging with snowmelt enveloped our bodies. The steep evergreen hills dropping to the river formed a spectacular background. The joyful laughter of rafters on the river echoed throughout the narrow valley. Our senses were on overload. It created a memorable cycling day.

Another frequently asked question we received was "Why?" Why did we, a couple in our mid-fifties, need to cross the country on bicycles? Our answer was simple: Adventure. Each day was a new adventure. Each day played out differently. Off the road, life was rote. Our lives had a daily pattern. As a couple in our mid-fifties we had already experienced so many of the wonderful firsts in life—welcoming a new baby into the family, starting our first jobs, buying our first home. On the road, life was a daily challenge. Each day was another first, and we loved it!

We remember our nine weeks together on the road as a special time in our lives. We needed each other for everything—for support, for sharing, for friendship, for love. Spending every hour of every day together made us cherish the relationship we have. We loved our daily rituals—David's hollering "Next" when it was my turn to get into the bathroom in predawn darkness, our high-fives at the conclusion of each day, and the daily discussion of David's statistics. Life on the road was simple. No meetings to attend, no phones to answer. We rolled along with our favorite person, grateful to be able to share the experience. We lived each day as two middle-aged cyclists who followed the philosophy, "You are only as old as you act." We climbed steep hills. We sped along smooth terrain. We put in one-hundred-mile days. We're not old because we cycled across the United States!

Appendix
Detailed Routing

For much of the bike trip, we used maps produced by Adventure Cycling of Missoula, Montana (www.adv-cycling.org, phone 800-755-2453). The organization has three cross-country routes: the TransAmerica Bicycle Trail (12 sectional maps) which starts in Astoria, Oregon and finishes in Yorktown, Virginia, the Northern Tier route (11 sectional maps) which begins in Anacortes, Washington and terminates in Bar Harbor, Maine, and the Southern Tier route (7 sectional maps) which starts in San Diego and finishes in St. Augustine, Florida. For our cross-country trip we biked Adventure Cycling's TransAmerica Bicycle Trail from Oregon to Yellowstone National Park, where we started using our own routes. When we crossed into Ohio, we returned to Adventure Cycling, using the final section of their Northern Tier Cross-Country Route—the Iowa to Maine Bicycle Route. The routing for each day is laid out, and if a printed source of the routing is available it is referenced.

Chapter 1: Coastal Ranges of Oregon

MAP

Day 1: Astoria, OR to Tillamook   TransAm : Section 1
US 101 all day

Day 2: Tillamook to Salem   TransAm: Section 1
US 101 – Neskawin
Rt. 18 – Valley Junction

Rt. 22 – Rickeall
Rt. 22 – Salem (busy road-see map for local diversion)

Day 3: Salem to Eugene TransAm: Section 1
Rt. 22 – Rt. 99W
Rt. 99W – Corvallis
Local Roads – Eugene, OR

Day 4: Eugene to Redmond TransAm: Section 2
Local roads – Walterville
Rt. 126 – McKenzie Bridge
Rt. 242 – Sisters
Rt. 126 – Redmond

Day 5: Redmond to Prineville TransAm: Section 2
Local Roads

Day 6: Prineville to John Day TransAm: Section 2

Day 7: John Day to Baker City TransAm: Section 2
Rt. 26 – Austin Junction
Rt. 7 – Baker City

Chapter 2: Rivers of Idaho

MAP

Day 1: Baker City to Cambridge, ID TransAm: Section 3
Rt. 86 – Oxbow
Rt. 71 – Cambridge

Day 2: Cambridge to Riggins TransAm: Section 3
Rt. 95 – Riggins

Day 3: Riggins to Kooskia TransAm: Section 3

Rt. 95 – Grangeville
Rt. 13 – Kooskia

Day 4: Kooskia to Lolo Hot Springs, MT   TransAm: Section 3

Day 5: Lolo Hot Springs to Missoula   TransAm: Section 3
Rt. 12 – Lolo
Rt. 12 – Missoula suburbs
Local roads – Missoula

Chapter 3: Big Sky Country

MAP

Day 1: Missoula to Sula   TransAm: Section 4
Local roads – suburbs
Rt. 93 – Lolo
Local roads – Florence
Rt. 203 – Rt. 269
Rt. 269 – Hamilton
Rt. 93 – Sula

Day 2: Sula to Dillon   TransAm: Section 4
Rt. 93 – Chief Joseph Pass
Rt. 43 – Wisdom
Rt. 278 – Rt. 222
Rt. 222 – Dillon

Day 3: Dillon – Virginia City   TransAm: Section 4
Rt. 41 – Twin Bridges
Rt. 287 – Virginia City

Day 4: Virginia City – W. Yellowstone   TransAm: Section 4
Rt. 287 – Ennis
Rt. 287 – W. Yellowstone

Day 5: W. Yellowstone – Cooke City, MT   Self-routing

Park roads – Madison
    -Norris
    -Canyon Village
    -Tower-Roosevelt
    -Cooke City

Day 6: Cooke City – Cody, WY   Self-routing
        Rt. 212 – Rt. 296
        Rt. 296 – Rt. 120
        Rt. 120 – Cody

Chapter 4: Cowboys

MAP

Day 1: Cody – Lovell   Self-routing
        Alt. 14 – Lovell

Day 2: Lovell – Sheridan   Self-routing
        Alt. 14 – Rt. 14
        Rt. 14 – Sheridan

Day 3: Sheridan – Gillette   Self-routing
        Rt. 126 – Buffalo
        Interstate 90 – Gillette

Day 4: Gillette – Spearfish, SD   Self-routing
        I-90 – Sundance
        Local road that parallels I-90 – Spearfish

Day 5: Spearfish – Rapid City   Self-routing
        I-90 - Sturgis
        I-90 – Blackhawk
        Local road (parallels I-90) – Rapid City

Chapter 5: Good Lands, Badlands

MAP

Day 1: Rapid City to Interior   Self-routing
   Rt. 44 – Interior

Day 2: Interior to Winner   Self-routing
   Rt. 44 – Winner

Day 3: Winner to Pickston   Self-routing
   Rt. 18 – Pickston

Day 4: Pickston to Yankton   Self-routing
   Rt. 46 – Wagner
   Rt. 50 – Yankton

Day 5: Yankton to Sioux City, IA   Self-routing
   Rt. 50 – Vermillion
   Rt. 50 – Westfield, IA
   Rt. 12 – N. Sioux City
   Bike path along river – Sioux City

Chapter 6: Corn...Corn...Corn

MAP

Day 1: Sioux City to Fort Dodge   Self-routing
   Rt. 20 – Early
   Rt. 7N – Rt. 15
   Rt. 15 – Rt. 7
   Rt. 7 – Fort Dodge

Day 2: Fort Dodge to Waterloo   Self-routing
   Local roads
   (Parallel Rt. 20) – Duncombe, Webster City
   Rt. D25 – Williams, Owasa

Rt. D35 – Hudson
Rt. 63 (busy road) – Waterloo
(Bike path parallels road near Waterloo)

Day 3: Waterloo to Galena, IL   Self-routing

Local roads
(Parallel Rt. 20)
Rt. D20 - Jesup
Rt. 939 – Rt. D22
Rt. D22 – Dyersville
Bike path – Dubuque
Rt. 20 (busy road) – Galena, IL

Day 4: Galena, IL to Bettendorf, IA   Self-routing

Rt. 20 – Rt. 84
Rt. 84 – Rt. 30
Rt. 30 – Clinton, IA
Rt. 67 – Bettendorf

Chapter 7: Canal Routes

Day 1: Bettendorf to Peru, IL   Self-routing

Local roads – Centennial Bridge
Rt. 67 – Airport Rd.
Airport Rd. – Rt. 6
Rt. 6 – Peru

Day 2: Peru to Bradley   Self-routing

Rt. 6 – Morris
Rt. 113 – Bradley

Day 3: Bradley to Logansport, IN   Self-routing

Rt. 17 – Rt. 1
Rt. 1 – Rt. 114

Rt. 114 – Indiana Border becomes Rt. 10
Rt. 10 – Roselawn
Rt. 110 – Rt. 143
Rt. 143 – Rt. 35
Rt. 35 – Logansport

Day 4: Logansport to Fort Wayne   Self-routing

Rt. 24 – Peru, IN
Alt. 24 – Wabash
Rt. 24 - Huntington
Local roads- Zonesville, Yoder, Ft. Wayne airport

Chapter 8: Buckeye State

MAP

Day 1: Fort Wayne, IN to Defiance, OH   Iowa-Maine: section 2

Local roads – Edgerton
Rt. 500 – Payne, OH
Rt. 500 – Paulding
Rt. 111 – Defiance

Day 2: Defiance to Bowling Green   Iowa-Maine: section 2

Rt. 424 – Napoleon
Rt. 110 – Grand Rapids
Local roads – Tontogany, Bowling Green

Day 3: Bowling Green to Oberlin   Iowa-Maine: section 2

Rt. 105 – Pemberville
Local roads – Oberlin

Day 4: Oberlin to Painesville   Iowa-Maine: section 2

Local roads – Brunswick
Local roads through Cleveland's Metro
Park system – Chagrin Falls
Local roads – Painesville

Chapter 9: Land of Many Lakes

MAP

Day 1: Painesville to Cambridge Springs, PA   Iowa-Maine: section 2

Local roads parallel to I-90
Local roads – Pierpont
Rt. 167 (OH)/Rt. 198 (PA) – Conneautville, PA
Rt. 18 – Springboro
Local roads – Rt. 98
Rt. 98 – Crossingville
Local roads – Cambridge Springs

Day 2: Cambridge Springs to Jamestown, NY   Iowa-Maine: section 2

Local roads – Corry, PA
Rt. 957 – Sugargrove, PA
Local road – Busti, NY   Self-routing
Local road – Jamestown

Day 3: Jamestown to Olean   Self-routing

Local road – Poland Center, NY
Local road – Waterboro
Rt. 242 – Little Valley
Rt. 353 – Salamanca
Local road parallels Rt. 17 – Olean, NY

Day 4: Olean to Corning   Self-routing

Local Rd. – Portville
Rt. 417 – Corning

Day 5: Corning to Geneva   Self-routing

Rt. 414 – Watkins Glen
Rt. 414 – Ovid
Rt. 96A – Geneva

Day 6: Geneva to Pulaski

Local roads – Seneca Falls   Self-routing

Local roads – Fair Haven   Iowa-Maine, Section 3
Local roads – Rt. 104A   Iowa-Maine, Section 3
Rt. 104A – Oswego   Self-routing
Rt. 104 – Rt. 104B
Rt. 104B – Rt. 3
Rt. 3 – Rainbow Shores on Lake Ontario (near Pulaski)

Day 7: Pulaski to Old Forge, NY

Rt. 13 – Pulaski   Self-routing
Local roads – Osceola   Iowa-Maine, Section 3
Local roads – West Leyden
Rt. 294 – Boonville
Local roads – Woodgate
Rt. 28 – Old Forge

Day 8: Old Forge – Saranac Lake

Local roads – Inlet   Iowa-Maine, Section 3
Rt. 28 – Blue Mountain Lake
Rt. 30 – Long Lake
Rt. 30 – Tuper Lake   Self-routing
Rt. 3 – Saranac Lake

Chapter 10: Home Again

MAP

Day 1: Saranac Lake to Middlebury, VT   Self-routing

Rt. 86 – Lake Placid, NY
Rt. 73 – Underwood
Rt. 9 – Severance
Rt. 74 – Ticonderoga
Ferry crossing of Lake Champlain
Rt. 74 – Rt. 30
Rt. 30 – Middlebury, VT

Day 2: Middlebury, VT to Lyme, NH   Iowa-Maine, section 4

Rt. 25 – Hancock, VT

Rt. 100 – Stockbridge
Rt. 107 – S. Royalton
Rt. 14 – Sharon
Rt. 132 – Thetford Center
Local roads – East Thetford
Local road- Lyme, NH

Day 3: Lyme – Conway, NH   Iowa-Maine, section 4

Rt. 10 – North Haverhill
Rt. 116 – Rt. 112
Rt. 112 – Lincoln
Rt. 112 – Conway, NH

Day 4: Conway, NH to Newcastle, ME   Iowa-Maine, section 4

Local roads – Fryburg, ME
Rt. 5 – Lovell
Local roads – Norway
Local roads – Turner
Local roads – Richmond
Local roads – Newcastle

Day 5: Newcastle to Camden, ME   Iowa-Maine, section 4

Rt. 1 – Waldoboro
Rt. 1 – Warren
Rt. 90 – Camden

Day 6: Camden to Bar Harbor, ME   Iowa-Maine, section 4

Rt. 52 – Belfast
Rt. 1 – Ellsworth
Rt. 230 – Trenton
Rt. 198 – Mount Desert
Rt. 233 – Bar Harbor, ME